What people are saying about...
"Dammit, I Learned a Lot from That Son-of-a-Gun"

"Wise and unforgettable, you'll be entranced by this journey back into the lives of these original voices on a search for truth. Reflecting on the moments when the world as they knew it came to an end, *Dammit*'s authors invite us to engage the same deep questions, emerging from the experience both wrung out and uplifted. These stories are as compulsively readable as popcorn in a scary movie!"

— *Sue Stauffacher,*
Author of Donuthead *and Other Children's Books*

"Siblings, creeps, fighters, strangers and friends who help us face the strangeness of life. These are the true characters in *Dammit* who show us, as one writer learns, that it's 'my responsibility to find the truth' and keep on going. These are all our stories. Read one, you'll come back for more."

— *Ron Steffens,*
Educator/Author/Forest Firefighter

"*Dammit, I Learned a Lot from That Son-of-a-Gun* is moving, funny and crisply written. All of us have met characters— some of whom had profound influence on us—and this collection will remind you of them and how they changed your life. It's a quick and riveting read, one with which you'll be happy to have spent time."

— *Drey Samuelson,*
U.S. Senate Chief of Staff

---

nt on who we are, and there's no escape from the p... you read these stories, you'll find yourself turning around, perhaps glancing over your shoulder. For there's another version of you, that lovable twin in all its glory. The one who lived, laughed, survived and eventually thrived."

— *Patricia Menick,*
Sculptor and Installation Artist

I Learned a
Lot from That
Son-of-a-Gun

BRANDT
STREET
PRESS

"Dammit, I Learned a Lot from That Son-of-a-Gun"

© 2014 by Brandt Street Press

Published by
Brandt Street Press
P. O. Box 8243
Pittsburgh, PA 15217-0243
www.brandtstreetpress.com

ISBN: 978-0-9742607-4-7

Library of Congress Control Number: 2014935301

Cover and Book Design by
Mike Murray
Pearhouse Productions
Pittsburgh, PA
www.pearhouse.com

Printed in the United States of America

A NOTE TO THE READER

Every son-of-a-gun in this book is different, but you'll recognize each one. We've all had them in our lives, these sons-of-guns. And whether we love them or we hate them, they are our teachers. They impart some kernel of truth that we carry with us always.

You may not know these people, but you will know these stories. They're about emotions we all feel—fear, anger, temptation, even those times you slap yourself on the forehead and call yourself an idiot. The circumstances may be different, but the pain, the heartache and the triumph, those remain true.

While the stories in this book are real, a detail may differ here or there. In certain cases, names were changed to protect the guilty.

Enjoy these stories, dammit!

The Editors

HONOR

Mike Connell

GARY AND I POSITIONED OUR TEN-YEAR-OLD SELVES IN THE SWEET SPOT—on the other side of two rows of cars, with just enough obstacles to momentarily slow any pursuers. It was a challenging yet manageable distance for a snowball.

We discovered this unique winter-time feature of the new Giant Eagle grocery store façade almost by accident. One or both of us had pelted it without much thought, seen the effect and quickly deduced the potential. The façade was slightly angled and was made of plastic or fiberglass or something else that made a pleasing hollow pop when hit just right. If there was a sticky snowfall, the façade would be covered with an inch or more of snow. People were constantly coming and going and, if we hit the façade at just the right moment, a person and their groceries would get a small avalanche from above, pretty much guaranteeing that they'd get snow all over themselves—down their collar, into their groceries, you name it.

It was a one-shot stunt, so timing really mattered. We had done it before, with devastating effect. A few times, the victims never put together how it happened.

On this particular day, we were waiting for the perfect victim. It was a long wait. Standing around in the parking lot stockpiling snowballs, we must have looked like the picture of mischief. We were loitering and up to no good in the classic sense. Gary had on his military-style green hooded snorkel coat and a cap. I was always jealous of his coat because it was so smooth that he could improvise at any moment and slide down a hill without needing a sled. I was wearing my Steeler jacket and my ski mask.

I loved my ski mask. It was burgundy and it had eye holes and a mouth hole. Once, walking home from Schenley Skating Rink, my older sister Jennie's friend Joe kept calling me Spiderman, relentlessly, with exaggerated Spiderman body language. It was part teasing and part admiration, and I took it both ways. I loved Spiderman. That mask was cool.

Eventually, Gary got impatient. He saw a man who was only about fifty feet from us, but he was on Loretta Street, which rises from the parking lot at an angle and is bounded by a twenty-foot retaining wall and a fence, so in effect he was much farther away. The man was waiting for the 56E Greenfield.

Gary headed off to the left and threw a perfect shot right in the center of the man's back. It had a nice arc to it. Not too hard, not too soft, like a perfectly executed free throw that ended in a swish. It made a soft plop as it hit right between the man's shoulder blades and left a sticky white bull's-eye on the man's dark overcoat.

The man turned immediately to look down at us. His pure white hair was now visible under his fedora. He had an angry, ruddy, wrinkled face. I voiced my disapproval to Gary, but he just shrugged and held out his hands in a gesture that meant "What're you gonna do?" He knew his mistake and didn't have to explain. He didn't know that it was an old man. He just saw that it was a man.

The old man began to yell profanity at us. Gary was too embarrassed so I walked over a little closer and yelled to the man that we were sorry, turned and walked back to our position, leaving the old man where he was.

Gary would never have hit that man with a snowball if he'd known he was old. That was understood between us and didn't have to be said out loud. We didn't hit old people with snowballs. That was one of our rules. The rules kept us from victimizing the wrong people. We didn't hit old people. We didn't hit kids who were younger than us. We didn't hit girls. Our rules also kept us honest, and kept us from going after low-hanging fruit. No buses or delivery trucks. Seriously, who can't hit a bus? And people didn't care about their work vehicles unless they owned them. And even then, these people were working. They were busy. Maybe we intuitively knew that a job makes people behave themselves. At least while they're working, usually.

The whole idea was to get people to chase us. We wanted them to chase us and fail to get us. That was important. If they could come close to getting us but be just unable to, that was the gold standard.

We were so guerrilla about this stuff that we always had an escape plan. We knew the neighborhood well enough that we knew which yards had fences and which ones led to the next street. We knew where unlocked garages and sheds stood for hiding places. We always had rendezvous sites for when we got separated. We had alternate rendezvous sites for when the first rendezvous sites didn't work out.

One time, we broke a rule, sort of. At the corner of Murray and Forbes in Squirrel Hill, we were pelting the passing cars with our snowballs. It was a slow day. Every once in a while, a car would slow down, but we got no real outrage in return. After a while, a bus driver stuck at a red light opened his driver's side window and warned us not to hit his bus with a snowball. Man, that was all we needed to hear. We wouldn't have even given him a look if he hadn't called our attention to him. I don't know how many snowballs we got into his window—onto him and his dashboard and his seat, onto his whole driver area—but it was beautiful.

I paid him no mind and was looking for our next victim when I saw Gary take off, and then I heard the huffing and puffing. It was the bus driver. He was fat, bald and angry, and he was less than five feet away and getting larger and larger. I bolted up Forbes after Gary and heard the bus driver's footsteps clopping and his lungs laboring in my wake. Every ten feet or so, I would look over my shoulder and see him not quite keeping up with me, until he finally relented at Little's Shoes, about four hundred yards from his bus. Not bad for a fat guy. I stopped and turned to look at him, out of breath myself. He was bent over, heaving up and down to get air into his lungs with his hands on his knees. He threatened to kill us if he ever caught us, and of course this made our laughter and ridicule and pointing and knee-slapping even worse.

He slowly turned and headed back to his bus, stopping every once in a while to pretend to chase us again when a particular insult or barb stung too much to let it slide, but he had no more run left in him, and we knew it. It took him a while to get back to his bus, which was left idling at the intersection. Seriously. He left his bus at the red light. How many driverless green lights did those passengers and those in the cars behind it have to suffer through while the bus driver went off to get revenge? Sometimes you have to wonder what's wrong with some people.

Looking back on it, we tended toward specific victims: males in middle age. Males in their twenties still scared us and could run fast. But men in their thirties were starting to mellow. They had begun to grow their paunches. They didn't have as much spring in their step. They had less need to prove themselves. I often think about that when I think about our country's Constitution. A man (or, in theory, a woman, but I doubt the framers even imagined it) is forbidden to be president until age thirty-five. Guys settle themselves down a lot by then. Women didn't scare us, but they weren't as funny when they were frustrated and angry. And women could *never* catch us. We knew that. No challenge. We didn't hit many women.

When it came to old people and younger kids, it was a bright line. We weren't bullies.

So on the day in question I was facing the Giant Eagle, still waiting for a suitable victim to landslide, when I got grabbed from behind by the back of my head. I never saw it coming. Someone had gotten a mix of my hair and my ski mask, and had begun punching me in the face. It was overwhelming. Who was doing this to me? I was mostly blinded, as the eye holes of my ski mask were off to the side by my ear. I couldn't escape the punches as they came one after the other, all to my face. They were sharp and hard. I was being manhandled. I was being pulled and shoved and thrown around by someone much stronger than me. I don't know for sure how long it lasted or even how many punches I took. It was more than five and probably less than fifteen.

Somehow I got the ski mask off my face and saw my attacker. It was the old man. After a few more incoming shots to my face, I managed to squirm free and wiggle away out of his reach. He made a move toward Gary but stopped immediately as Gary backed away.

The old man shook a fist, and I saw liver spots on his knuckles. He seemed content to let us cower away, so Gary and I slinked off together, looking back occasionally to make sure he hadn't changed his mind and decided to deliver some more hurt. We needn't have bothered. He walked to the bus stop, never giving us another glance.

After that, we headed to Homer's Gas Station to use the bathroom. I wanted to look at my face. I was certain that something was broken, but I wasn't sure what. So many places were wet and stinging and throbbing and swelling.

I had two swollen black eyes. My nose was bleeding so that it made me look like I had a blood goatee. My cheeks were blotchy and red and swollen, and they were tender to the touch. My lips were pink and blue and purple. They looked like they had blueberries and grapes attached to them. Fortunately, my teeth were all still intact.

The eye and mouth holes of my ski mask were misshapen and no longer resembled a face. The area between each eye, and between the eyes and the mouth, had been stretched thin, and the elastic around the mouth opening was showing through. The shape of the mask no longer looked like it was for a head. The front of the mask was caked with gooey nose blood. No more Spiderman mask. It was garbage.

Gary and I had a thing where we wouldn't cry in front of each other, no matter how jacked up we got. If we fell off our skateboards, wrecked our bikes, anything like that, we held it in until it passed.

I was definitely crying in that bathroom. But I don't think it was from pain. When I was getting punched, I thought I was simply losing a fight to an older kid who had suckered me. I was genuinely shocked to discover that it wasn't a bigger kid. Getting beat up, unreservedly, by a grown man was out of my experience. Lots of adults hit, but they usually slapped or cuffed or shoved or backhanded or something like that. This man had wound up and thrown real punches with his full weight behind them.

I washed my face, gingerly, with the gas station's cold-water-only option. Gary and I didn't say much to each other about it, and it went without saying that we wouldn't be telling our parents, or any adults for that matter. That was understood.

Even after washing up, my face was still a mess. I spent a lot of time and energy trying to hide it, but when my dad saw me later that night, he asked me if I had gotten into a fight. I told him no, I'd wrecked head-first while sled riding. I had used that explanation before when I got into a fight that I didn't want him to know about. It was a plausible thing to have happened to me at that time in my life, and he accepted it without much comment.

For a long time, I never spoke of it. But I often think about that old man. Who was he? Was he the grand-father of a friend? Was he a friend of my own grandpar-ents? Was he on his way home from work? Or from the doctor's? Was he the Pittsburgh Golden Gloves cham-pion of 1933? Did he go home, eat a TV dinner and ask himself, "What on earth got into me?" Or maybe he was just disappointed that he couldn't knock out a ten-year-old.

Whatever his story, I imagine now that he was the type of guy who spent his life demanding respect and getting it, one way or the other. Maybe in the world that he grew up in, that was the best option. Face down any slight or insult, or expect more of the same. But he would never have seen us again in his life if he had just let it pass, so maybe he lacked perspective about that. I may never know. He would be in his early hundreds by now, so it's likely he's a half mile away in Calvary Cemetery.

My son is now nine years old. He's already bigger and stronger than I was at ten. Still, I know and work with many men in their sixties. He's no match for them.

Plus, I don't want him to behave like I did at all. Even if he has a "code" guiding his actions and helping him select his targets with some form of moral regard, I hope he has the sense that choosing victims is still inherently the act of a scoundrel.

Did you know the old man? Maybe you're reading this and heard it from his side of things. Maybe you visit his grave because he was important to you. If you do, tell him I'm sorry. I said it to him that day, but I don't think it made it through. I really don't want him to think I'm still a jerk.

*Mike Connell is a married father of two and has lived his whole life in Pittsburgh. He's an exercise physiologist who works in clinical training, where he helps people lose weight, quit smoking and manage stress. He has been interviewed in many Pittsburgh publications and has appeared on local news programs concerning well-ness. Through the years, Mike has also worked as a movie usher, janitor, box boy, videographer, video store clerk and printer. He has done location scouting, voice work, and sound Foley on a full-length independent film shot in Pittsburgh. Mike is an avid reader of many genres and also a fan of all types of films, but he is an avid fan of horror movies. As a related hobby, he builds homemade Halloween yard props, such as dummies, mummies and tombstones. His collection of Silver Age Marvel comics is nothing to sneeze at, either.*

JAILHOUSE MAIL

Bill Collins

JEANETTE SENT ME A LETTER FROM JAIL back in May of '75, where she was doing nine months on a plea bargain for sale of heroin. In her letter my big sis, five years older than me, touched on many topics I wish I would've been able to address at that time, but I was just 17—with all the know-it-allness that comes with that age—and was not able to respond effectively in the way she needed me to.

As a matter of fact, I never responded at all….

Bill,

Hey Dude what's up? Long time no see, eh? Heard you've been really busy with school and working. I'll bet you still find time to throw in some partying though ☺ I'm glad

*to hear you've really got it together. This card
is implying your forthcoming trip with your
school and also lending hope to your wish for
that big trip to the Philippines and wherever
else your spacey mind may take you.*

Now that I'm a so-called grownup, I'm trying to figure out how come I never wrote back or went to visit her during the time she was locked up.

*It's good to know you're not following in
my footsteps cause quite a few of mine have
excrement on them and it's too late to clean up
the mess.*

The envelope that contained a no-name greeting card titled EVERYONE HAS ALWAYS SAID YOU WOULD GO FAR in honor of my high school graduation was lovingly decorated using about ten different colors of fine-point artist markers. The top edge of the back side of the envelope had a row of LSD-inspired psychedelic images: a cluster of multicolored hearts, planets, fantastic faces on animal bodies, disembodied floating eyes intertwined with letters that spelled out hidden words.

When I squinted my eyes and focused really hard, I made out, under a smiling red demon wielding a pitchfork in one hand and flashing the V sign with the other, the words "The Devil Made Me Do It." The word "Spaced" wound its way through the Saturn motif on the far left, next to what looked like a Mardi Gras clown mask.

The adult version of me can now appreciate the thought and time that went into the decoration and thinks: "This envelope was decorated not only by someone who truly loved me, but someone for whom the length of those endless days must've been challenging to fill."

The 17-year-old version of me didn't think much about it at all. I think part of that teenager was mad at her. First of all for not keeping well enough in touch before being busted, secondly for getting caught, and thirdly for missing my graduation! My 17-year-old self sure felt smug and enlightened enough back then, but looking back I know now I still had a lot to learn about empathy.

I can picture her now in her cell or dorm room, or wherever they stuck her—a petite, high-cheekboned *mestiza* beauty bending over my card as she decorates it, brow furrowed in concentration. Maybe the tip of her tongue sticking out the side of her mouth, like it used to when she drew. Maybe she's unconsciously brushing wisps of her long, bottle-blonde hair out of her eyes as she wields her pen.

> *Well I've shed my old shoes and am ready for a*
> *whole new trek. I'm anticipating my release into*
> *that wonderful and sometimes gruesome world*
> *out there, sometimes referred to as the "streets."*
> *To take up my time and to condition my body*

and mind for my rebirth, I'm practicing Yoga.
It's amazing how well I feel even in a place such
as this rathole.

I can almost picture myself back then as a long-haired version of Beavis or Butthead thinking something like: "Yoga, cool. Jail, dumb. Whatever.... I'll see her when she gets out." Just taking her—and life—for granted, I guess.

I had big plans, sort of. Inspired by the slideshow of a guest teacher at the hippie alternative school I attended—all green fields, bamboo forests and palm trees—I was gonna make my way to the Philippine Islands and travel from village to village like he did, making street music on my guitar with the local musicians. Cool. No college for me. Trying to shock my mom in a rebellious moment, I told her: "You know what? I'm not even gonna *go* to college."

"It's good you say that," she replied in her German accent, shocking me instead. "Because I don't have the money to send you."

When my mother went to visit my sister at Elmwood Correctional Institute in Milpitas, I'm sure she filled Jeanette in about my crazy teenage goings-on and plans. At least the ones she was privy to. Why I never accompanied her to see my sister in jail, I can't rightly say. Part of the reason, I guess, was that since I didn't yet drive, I'd have to go with my mother. And because Mom seemed to be getting crazier with every passing year, for the sake of my own mental health, I stayed away from her as much as possible. Maybe I was freaked out about going into a scary place of incarceration, or maybe I was just plain being teenage lazy.

She invited me, asked me, gently expressed her disappointment, but never laid a guilt trip on me or was mean about my contribution to her isolation.

> *I was really looking forward to seeing you this weekend, but am happy just the same that you have some productive plans and ideas. I have so many things to rap to you about, Bill, I would have to write a book to let you know what's been happening.*

I'm sure now it must've been a dagger in my sister's heart every visiting day her "Little Bro" didn't show up. If only I knew then what I know now about loneliness, isolation and the value of contact with those that are most important to us. Yet even in her gentle rebuke to me she stayed positive, never pointing the finger of blame. She just laid out what she needed from me, and I ignored it.

The craziest part of all is that, now that all these years have passed, I would really have loved to read that book about the part of her life I never gave her the opportunity to share with me. As I sit now with pen in hand, I guess what I'm doing is trying to write that book myself, since she's no longer around to tell her own story.

I would really dig rapping with you and sharing our philosophies concerning this trip called life. Believe me, doing time is a rip-off, and I have no intention of blowing it when there are so many things out there I'm eager to try. I wish you would drop me a line now and then to turn me on to what's happening to you. You realize that Mom's not always aware as to what you're really up to.

No...Mom never knew about me hopping that freight train north; or that little junket to Texas my tenth-grade summer to cop those keys of weed; or the time my first love, Julie, almost died slipping and cracking her head wide open on the pavement, chasing after me following a drunken breakup in Walnut Creek. No...Mom never knew, but Jeanette did.

Now, looking back 36 years since we parted, sometimes it seems as though the closeness my sister and I shared through our childhoods and some of our teen years—before she got married and moved off—was only a false memory. Finding her letter to me in a dusty box of keepsakes was a lot like opening a treasure chest and finding a golden nugget inscribed *validation*. We were connected in a genuine way. And we still are.

I take a special interest in you as my brother and one of my closest and dearest friends, so fly a kite in my direction, y'hear?

Optimistic to the end, once again she invited me to reach out and make contact with her.

> *When you write, I'll certainly make it a point to answer in a more voluminous and enlightening manner.*

And then she lets me off the hook, not pushing me too hard, encouraging me at the end to succeed in my life outside—a place she could only daydream of at that time.

> *Anyway, if I don't hear from you, I wish you luck in your trip and your forthcoming enterprise as a musician.*

> *Dig you Later,*
> *Love ya,*
> *Jeanette*

Despite having no intention of "blowing it" when she finished serving her sentence, that's exactly what she did. Her release from jail marked the beginning of her end. Troubles at home with her increasingly violent and controlling husband drove her back onto those "sometimes gruesome streets," where she made money in illicit, illegal ways and got right back on junk. Seriously, this time. February 1, 1977, a year and a month after her release and three months before her twenty-fifth birthday, her short life came to a tragic end.

As far as I know, the police never did much towards finding her killer—after all, by their reckoning, she was just another dead junkie. The detective my mom spoke to made some remark about *"those* kind of people...."￼ The investigation never went anywhere. Her killer was never caught.

There was a postscript to her letter:

> *P.S. I wish I could be at your graduation but considering the circumstances, you'll just have to act as if and know I'd be there if I could.*

Dear Jeanette,

I'm so sorry it took me so long to write back. I wish I would've known how to be a better friend, and how to come through for you those times you reached out to me. I miss you and think of you at least once every day. I know you'd be here for me if you could. I do try to act as if you are still here and in a way I hope you'd be proud of.

> Dig you Forever,
> Love ya too,
> Bill

&

In 1976, **Bill Collins** played his first gig as a professional musician. Since then, he's played punk squats and clubs all over the U.S. and Europe, in bands with names like Millions of Dead Cops, and Fang. He's played cowboy bars in Montana, Irish pubs in Connecticut, Union rallies and picket lines up and down the East Coast—even recorded a couple of LPs in Nashville. For most of Bill's life, songwriting is what scratched his storytelling itch. These days, he's seeing what it feels like to strip away the music and the rhymes, leaving just the stories. After 20 years in New Haven, Connecticut, Bill once again resides in Berkeley, California, where he's making music, teaching guitar and working on his first book, a memoir focused on his big sis, Jeanette. You can learn more about Bill at www.billcollinsguitar.com.

STEEL TOWN DANCING QUEEN

Judi Resick-Csokai

"YOUNG LADY, GET YOUR *DERRIERE* OUT OF THAT CHAIR!" boomed a voice from behind me.

Maryetta's wispy black hair swayed in the breeze from the fan. Her stern glance revealed the lines in her timelessly beautiful face. Her words commanded a silence that only her little black pug dared to break. Gypsy skittered across the dance floor, her clicking toenails like tiny tap shoes, and stood guard by her angry mistress.

I was mortified—not because Maryetta reprimanded me in front of the ten-year-olds who I, a twelve-year-old, was leading in warm-ups at the barre, but because I had the nerve to sit down in front of her. Maryetta had taught me how to moonwalk and how to do a split. At 76, she could still do both.

After class, I went to her dim-lit office. I stood there for a few moments before she looked down at me through her reading glasses, even though she was sitting. "I'm sorry," I whispered, biting my lip. I avoided eye contact and instead glanced at the ballerina poster behind her. The caption read: *To dream it is to believe it...to achieve it is to become it.* I thought of how Maryetta had once told me she doctored up that ballerina with some black tempera paint because she thought the lighting and angle of the photo were unflattering to the poor dancer's body.

"It's not just about teaching the kids the steps, you know," she said, shaking her head. "You have to be an example to them. And you can do better. You know that. Now please go get me a BLT and a chicken bouillon with hot water before the next class."

She handed me three dollars, and I ascended from the basement dance studio out to the streets of the dilapidated Steel Valley. My heart raced and I fought back tears. It was that same feeling that I always got when she was forthright with me. She was more blatantly honest than anyone else in my life. I loved her and I despised her for that. I ran down the street past the fire station and the line at the soup kitchen to the corner diner. She was right: I could do better. I would never let her down again.

Maryetta Evans had been part of a foursome family vaudeville act in the 1930s and 1940s. During World War II, she and her family went overseas to entertain the troops. Originally from the Steel Valley just outside Pittsburgh, the family later returned to the area and ran a dance studio in Homestead, Pennsylvania.

I first met Maryetta in 1983—the year *Flashdance* hit the theaters, steel mill layoffs started, and hormones attacked me. Puberty is awkward, but it's especially wicked when it cuts short your childhood, making you an ogre next to the other kids your age. Earlier that year, I had been a victim of the cheese maze at Chuck E. Cheese, having managed to get stuck in one of the mouse holes at a birthday party. I would soon learn that there were no Holy Communion dresses in the tri-state area that would fit me. I was only seven years old.

I suspect my mom thought enrolling me in dance class would be a confidence booster. There were plenty of dance studios around town run by women who embraced 1980s fashion and other modern trends— but my parents were too earthy for the *froufrou*-ness of mall hair and fake nails on toe shoes. Ballet academies, with their strict dress codes and tightly-wound-bun approach to teaching children, were likely too formal and intimidating. So when a friend of the family told us of a former vaudeville entertainer running a dance studio out of a basement in the Steel Valley, we enthusiastically signed up.

My Wednesday evenings soon included a bacon cheeseburger and fries at Wendy's, followed by an hour of ballet and an hour of tap. As I descended into the studio, the stuffy sulfuric air of the steel town gave way to a cool, damp subterranean time capsule permeated by the faint scent of Chanel No. 5. The walls and wicker furniture in the waiting room were painted a dull black. Dusty Degas sketches of meaty ballerinas and pictures of tap dancers from another time (when sequins and top hats ruled) donned the walls. Black-and-white photos of marquees touting "Tonight—The Evans Four" hovered above a crowd of kids and parents of all colors, sizes and backgrounds who read crumpled, outdated magazines and barely acknowledged our arrival.

I started out in the six- to eight-year-old class, which seemed appropriate since I was seven years old. But I was the biggest.

After a few classes, Maryetta pulled my mom and me aside, which felt a lot like heading to a school principal's office.

"You're tall," she said. "Since this is your first year, you will stay in this class. But if you work hard, I'll move you up two classes next year."

I learned my steps. I never missed a class. As recital time neared, I was so excited to wear a costume. But to my horror, the costume we had ordered—the biggest size they had—did not fit. I blushed and started to cry. Maryetta pulled me aside.

"Come see me after class," she whispered, with a gentle touch to my shoulder.

Maryetta invited my mom and me to her house. She measured me and pulled out an old bathing suit, some tulle and a string of sequins. I watched as a costume sprung from her graceful grandmotherly hands. It was perfect.

"Next year I'll put you in class with the older girls. But you have to work hard," she said as she handed me the creation.

Over the summer, I grew. I was eight years old and bigger than my 16-year-old babysitter.

That fall, I enrolled in the pre-teen classes and danced alongside junior-high girls. Maryetta put me in the third row, which was perfectly fine by me. I hid out back there and kept to myself, often with my mind wandering off. For three years, I contentedly stood behind the leggy redhead and persnickety blonde, perfecting *chaînés* turns, tapping in two-inch heels (the one time I was happy to have feet too big for shoes like the other kids my age), and practicing knee slides to Barry Manilow's "Copacabana."

All was well in the third row until shortly after I turned 11. It was a few weeks before the annual recital at the Holiday House, an old Pittsburgh venue not unlike some forgotten Las Vegas club. We were practicing our jazz routine to Michael Jackson's "Don't Stop 'Til You Get Enough" when Maryetta stopped the music and made a beeline for me. In front of everyone she said, "You're not keeping up. Listen—you can't be a dancer if you are going to be overweight like this. It's holding you back. I know you can do better."

No one had ever been so direct with me. I finished the class feeling like my head was detached from my body. I went home and wept. My parents consoled me and told me that I could quit if I wanted to. I don't remember what made me go back. I like to think that it was spite. I would show her. She wouldn't make me quit that easily. But I'm pretty sure it had more to do with the brand-new cancan costume in my closet. I made it through the recital in the third row. I didn't smile—in fact I made sure that I scowled. I hated Maryetta.

That summer, I thought about dance and how I aspired to be in the Duquesne University Tamburitzans, a professional dance ensemble and the longest-running multicultural song and dance company in the U.S. As much as her words hurt me, I thought a lot about what Maryetta had said. I realized that she was not being mean, but honest. My parents helped me to understand that Maryetta's advice wasn't so much geared towards being skinny for the sake of being skinny, but rather towards embodying self-control and self-discipline, which are vital to dance. I gave up bacon cheeseburgers and started Weight Watchers. I lost twenty pounds and shot up a few inches. And I returned to the basement dance studio that fall.

"Oh my God! You came back!" Maryetta shouted across the dance floor. "And look at you—you completely transformed!"

"It was brutal what I said," she later admitted. "But it was because I knew you could do better. I would not have said that to someone I didn't believe in, you know."

That year, I moved up to the class with high school kids and adult women. She asked me to help out by running warm-ups for the younger classes. The steps and routines became more complicated, as did Maryetta's lessons.

"My mother used to show me a tap step one time," she would tell us. "If I didn't learn it, she would walk away and not talk to me all day. I let you off easy, showing you many times."

One girl in the class brought her boyfriend to watch us. In front of everyone, Maryetta said, "Sex and love are two different things if you think of it, really. Don't confuse the two. It will only bring you misery."

To the woman who slouched in the wicker chair scarfing down a bag of chips and waiting for class to start, she simply said, "Dance is what elevates us from apes."

Her brother Lester, who co-owned the studio and taught tap, died the following year. With the closing of the steel mill, enrollment dropped. The Holiday House closed. The steel-town streets became more dangerous and dire. In 1991, Maryetta broke the news to us all—she would retire to Florida. Our last recital was held at the more subdued Carnegie Library of Homestead music hall. Maryetta still donned her salmon-colored sequin suit and tapped. We all cried.

Before she left Pittsburgh, she accompanied me to a new dance studio that she had recommended. She watched me take a sample class and afterwards told me, "Honey, I think you're going to be just fine. Do keep in touch and let me know if you make it to that dance group you always aspired to be in."

I kept up my dancing and thought of her often. I made it into the Tamburitzans, and she came to a show my freshman year in West Palm Beach, Florida. She brought me flowers and we went out to dinner. She talked about her new gig as a lead dancer in a local troupe of women dancers over 50, the Palm Springs Follies, and confided that she would turn 83 soon.

"I remember that I was hard on you because I knew you could do better. And you got the message," she said.

That visit was the last time I saw her. She would go on to become the Guinness Book of World Records' World's Oldest Professional Show Dancer in 1999 at age 86. She passed away in 2009 at age 96.

I still dance. Having met my husband while dancing, it permeates my family's life to the point that we will travel ten hours by car on a weekend just to attend a dance event. And when I grow slack or lazy in dancing (or anything else in life), I always hear Maryetta say, "You can do better, you know that."

ॐ

*When **Judi Resick-Csokai** was a rotund, awkward child living upwind of the waning 1980s Pittsburgh steel-mill glory, she secretly wrote vignettes about characters in far-off places like Transylvania, Patagonia and the steppes of Central Asia, and hid them in the ripped seams of her knock-off Cabbage Patch Kid. Writing has always been a compulsion of sorts for Judi, and her passion for the written word translated into a job early on—in middle and high school, she delivered newspapers and even won the coveted Paper Carrier of the Year award twice. Growing up, Judi also spent countless hours studying classical and Eastern European folk dancing and music. From 1994-98, she performed and travelled extensively with the Duquesne University Tamburitzans while completing her undergraduate studies in nursing. She has worked in health care and research in Pittsburgh, Maryland and overseas, all the while continuing to write. Judi has published several essays and completed her first novel,* Circle of the Silver Birch Trees, *in 2014. She lives with her husband, Attila, and their two children in Pittsburgh, Pennsylvania.*

BEAUTY SCHOOL BIMBO

Katherine Gross

I WAS 32 YEARS OLD WHEN I DECIDED TO GO to beauty school. I had spent years giving my friends makeovers—a haircut here, a newly made-up face there—and my skills had me at those same friends' weddings later on, to prep their faces for the big day. I was also interested in skincare and beauty products—always looking for a miracle serum or the perfect shade of lipstick. I would spend hours at the library reading fashion magazines. I worshipped beauty, and so, at a crossroads in my professional life, beauty school seemed like a natural choice.

This happened to also be at a time when I had trouble trusting my instincts. I was a stranger to my own inner voice. I routinely ignored it and, to me, it was as though I didn't have one to begin with: that was how distant I was from it. I would do and say things only to appease others, and in this way I ignored what my gut was telling me to do or say. I was so busy trying to please people, I had no idea what my inner voice even sounded like.

There was a girl of Chinese descent in my beauty school class who tested this mistrust. Her name was Lulu. If I was the straight-A student, Lulu was the delinquent. I came to class on time; Lulu was almost always late. I asked questions and studied for tests; Lulu sat sullen and disinterested in what was going on around her. Where I was somewhat prim and proper in the way I spoke, Lulu was vulgar and inappropriate. I disliked her and didn't respect her in any way.

On her first day of class, Lulu lit an electronic cigarette during the anatomy lesson, and when the teacher told her to put it away, she half-closed her eyes, took a long drag and exhaled slowly. "Whas wrong?" she said. "Is only wata vapors. Is not real smoke."

The teacher was nonplussed. "Put it away or get a zero for the day and go home."

Lulu sighed and dropped the offending thing into her purse, then crossed her arms, shifted back into her seat and yawned.

The next day, we gathered around Liza, a willing student who acted as the waxing guinea pig for the rest of us. She held the pant leg of her scrubs up to her knee, and we watched the teacher apply the wax in a downward motion, press the strip onto the waxed area, and pull up and away. Liza's leg hair was now embedded into the pink wax on the strip, her skin smooth and shiny. We all spoke at once. "Did it hurt?" "Wow, look at those black bulbs at the end of the hairs!" "Those are the follicles."

Then Lulu piped up. "What if I want to wax my boyfwent's bawls?"

There was dead silence. What choice did we have? We burst into raucous laughter. We laughed at her in public and criticized her in private: *Who would say something like that aloud? Only a really crazy girl.*

Lulu's intentions, we eventually found out, were entirely based on her mother's desire to own a salon and use Lulu as the key to legitimate practice. Lulu's mother was Chinese and spoke no English. Since Lulu did speak English (albeit poorly), it was with great resentment that she attended beauty school in her mother's stead. At 19, Lulu had no desire to spend her summer cooped up in some fluorescent-lit classroom that smelled of old pizza and hair potion. Of course she had no respect for what the rest of us were doing: she wanted to be on the beach, covered in baby oil and surrounded by her many paramours. On our lunch breaks, Lulu would speak nonchalantly, but always disparagingly, of the many men in her life, mostly older and married, who bought her dinner and gifts. One almost felt sorry for the rascals, listening to the way Lulu collected them and tossed them aside.

One day, my disdain for Lulu became immediately personal. Little did I know that I was about to learn something important from her. A hot afternoon and a greasy lunch had made me queasy and tired, and so Lulu's offer to drive me home was a welcome one. Any offer of a ride was a saving grace to me—the heat was unbearable that summer, and taking public transportation held as much magic for me as a trip through hell. I dreaded going home each day. Riding the T train for twenty minutes to be dropped off in the dusty hubbub of downtown, only to get back on a noisy bus filled with people in stop-and-go traffic, was a true chore for me. I was an extremely impatient person. I hated waiting: on line at the bank, on line *anywhere*. Waiting did nothing to improve my mood. Although I did it most days, I would have done almost anything to avoid the two-hour commute home.

I'd been Lulu's passenger before without incident, and I climbed into her Infiniti gratefully. She listened to Top 40 music and drove a little fast and erratically, but these were trifles as long as I got home in one piece. As we buckled our seatbelts (or rather, I buckled my seatbelt; Lulu would never wear hers), I tried to make polite conversation. She talked about her various boyfriends and her dog, a Bichon named Cheng Cheng.

"I luv her so much. She sooooooo cute! My stupit roommate say she ate one of her Manolos but she the one who lef it out in the kitchen where Cheng Cheng was sure to get at it! She should have lef it in her room."

I listened and murmured my assent from somewhere far away. If I was Tokyo, Lulu was London. With each mile that went by, I was that much closer to safety and normalcy.

"I ha to drop you off at Wightman today, not all da way to your house, okay? I ha to go to wuhk at Keltic Kilt tonight."

Keltic Kilt was a strip club barely concealed as a bar. "Why do you work there? Isn't it filled with disgusting old men?"

"Is not so bad. I get a lot of good tip because I can look like an Asian schoolgirl. And my boyfwent like it."

I felt sorry for Lulu when I heard that. But she seemed fine with it—the whole thing: her designer bags, her multiple boyfriends, being treated as an object.

We had just pulled onto West Liberty Boulevard when I heard it. A sort of double-thump, rhythmic and faster as the car picked up speed.

"Do you hear that?" I said. "It sounds like the wheel." I had never owned my own vehicle and spoke with the timidity of an unenlightened child.

Lulu explained. "Oh. My ex-boyfwent fix it las week."

"He fixed the wheel?"

"Yeah. I think he did."

The sound persisted.

"He's a mechanic?"

"No. He a doctor."

I sat there and listened to the wheel thump. If it was her *ex*-boyfriend, perhaps the wheel hadn't been fixed in the proper sense. But Lulu seemed filled with faith. "If he fix a bone, he can fix a wheel."

The thumping grew worse as we sped toward the highway. There was no doubting, at this point, that it was the wheel. I pondered what to do, but years of being a silent, dependent passenger and that old desperate desire to not have to take public transportation loomed inside me.

"Lulu. We need to pull over."

Silence. (Except for the thumping, of course.)

"Wets jus turn up the music so we won't have to heaw it," she said and reached toward the volume and cranked it up.

"*...till you love me, Papa-Paparazzi...,*" Lady Gaga was screaming, and the wheel now not only thumped but rattled alarmingly.

Lulu sat and drove along, singing aloud. "Papa RAZZI...."

And so I sat and prayed.

We finally turned onto Wightman, a residential street near my house. We made a right turn and, as we did, the car came to a halt. I found myself sitting crookedly, my body at an awkward angle.

"What da fak?" Lulu squealed. "Wai here. Don't get up!"

I sat in silence, enraged at Lulu for putting me in this situation, but mostly at myself for staying in it. I could have asked Lulu to pull over and gotten out of the car immediately after we had left the parking lot at school. I could have sat on a safe, quiet, air-conditioned train, then taken a bus from downtown and walked the few blocks home. Sure, it would have taken a while longer, but I would have saved myself this brush with disaster. If I had trusted my own intuition, I would have saved myself a half hour of frantic, lonely fear and anxiety.

Now, I listened to my best instincts. I unbuckled my seatbelt and got out of the car. Lulu had disappeared. I looked around and saw her running daintily across the street in pursuit of the tire, which had rolled through a luckily empty intersection.

Soon, Lulu came walking back with the tire and laid it against the back door of the car. She was already on her cell.

"You SAY it was fix. Da whee fewl off!"

Silence.

"Yeah? We see who is laughing when I see you nex an punch you in da bawls! We see what will be rolling across street then! You will pay for dis you assho!"

She hung up.

At that very moment, a BMW pulled up.

"Das my boyfwent. Byeeee!" said Lulu, and she climbed into the BMW and drove away.

I am, after a year, just now learning how to hear the sounds of my own inner voice. It will take longer for me to trust it fully, but this incident proved to me that sometimes it's better to trust what I'm feeling about a situation than to trust what someone else says about it. Safer, too.

❧

Katherine Gross is a writer who enjoys spending time reading, running and cross-country skiing. The only dog she truly loves is Maisie, her stepmother's canine companion. She is not an animal person and has a dreaded fear of raccoons. Because of this, she doesn't like to take out the trash on summer nights. She lives in Pittsburgh, Pennsylvania.

THE OFFER

Douglas Gwilym

ONE OVERCAST LATE-SPRING AFTERNOON, I chose to invest the time I had in walking from my little bit of subletted apartment across Frick Park to the cool and attractive chain bookstore in Squirrel Hill. I'd come to Pittsburgh for a reason no less powerful and no more complex than "for love." I'd left my job and moved into the city without a strong plan or permanent employ-ment, but I was carrying the essentials around with me: I knew myself pretty well and was making a little prog-ress every day toward what I felt were reasonable goals.

That particular afternoon, I was to have three glori-ous hours in the bookstore, following my random literary and informational whims, and I didn't take it for granted. After, I was to meet my girlfriend and my roommate (two different people) for good Thai food and conversation.

Inside, I wandered for a few minutes, until I felt that familiar magnetic pull toward a short aisle with "Self Help" on one side and "Writing" on the other. I leaned against one side of the aisle, with my back against a shelf, and quickly lost myself to story structure, writers' markets and that great shibboleth: "Where do you get your ideas?"

It was an odd scrape-and-tap sound that brought me out of this self-induced trance. I tried to settle back in, but there was more scraping and tapping. I looked up.

A man was working his way up the aisle, leaning on a silver walker. He was heavy-set, hunched and balding, but those weren't the first things I noticed. I don't think they were what anyone noticed first about Isaac. He was wearing a thick, black pair of eyeglass frames, round and bold and ambiguously retro. They sat not-so-very squarely on his plump face and appeared to have only one intact lens. The other was an interlocking puzzle of broken glass, with open space between the shards.

He seemed to have somewhere to go, so I simply stepped out of the aisle and waited for him to pass.

He beamed at me, and this brought a great, electric transformation to his face. Straggles of ash-and-white hair stood clean off his scalp with it. He came a few more steps—scrape-tap, scrape-tap—and stopped, a great impassible cork in the bottle of "Writing and Self Help."

"I'm Isaac," he said, "and you're the first person today who's shown me basic human kindness."

He then began to talk. There was an impish lilt to his voice, but it also had a quality that was inherently fascinating, like the voice of one of those classic character actors who can make a reading of the phone book interesting. The books around us seemed to thrum with the energy of the guy's voice. I realized with some amusement I was having a real *Rime of the Ancient Mariner* moment, grabbed by the lapels and made to hear a tale, but it was bizarre: he quickly ran the conversational gamut from film and literature to Pittsburgh and cooking and world politics. I was physically uncomfortable, perched between shelves as I was, but there was no room between his sentences to ask if we could find a place to sit down, and besides, I was having an experience.

He started with assumptions. Was I new to the city? He felt that I must be. Did I have no steady job? The evidence of my presence in the bookstore in the middle of the afternoon was, he felt, confirmation enough. Sometimes I was allowed little personal riffs, but Isaac was an impassioned speaker. He was like professors I'd had, like people I'd seen on TV. He was a man with *joi de vivre,* and he was pushing the conversation, I slowly became aware, toward something very specific.

During a lull, he smirked and gave me an appraising look. "You're wondering why I wear these." He flicked the temple of the dark frames. "They're a reminder," he said.

Four years prior, he'd been crossing the street in another neighborhood. He'd looked both ways, but the car had come fast, from a side street, and had struck him going forty miles an hour.

His body, he said, had been broken in a dozen places, and he'd nearly died. He'd spent five months in a coma. This, combined with his long afflictions from a form of leukemia, left him in need of the walker. He wore the glasses just as they had been found on the pavement, to remind him of how fragile life is and how quickly it can get away from you.

"I know they make me look crazy, but I'm not." He wiggled his fingers through the open air on either side of the glasses and grinned. "Contact lenses," he explained. "So I don't forget."

The topics were so various, so apparently tangential—now talk of an estranged family, next the tale of his time in publishing in the '50s (a handful of science-fiction novels he'd written had apparently seen print)—that the hands of the clock on the wall nearby made multiple passes at each other before I could stop them. He had the preacher's and the politician's way of reading you. When you neared your tolerance threshold—perhaps it was when you shifted your weight x number of times or pursed your lips too noticeably—he knew, instinctively, that now was the time to take it up a notch.

In this way, we progressed from Isaac the young entrepreneur to Isaac the creative professional to Isaac the Washington politician…to Isaac the benefactor.

"It is in my power," he said, "to help a few young people out. You clearly have a good heart. I would like to see what you would do, if you were freed from financial and everyday concerns, to make the world a better place.

"When I was your age, someone did something similar for me, and I am simply trying to return the favor. I hope that *you*," he brought the assertion home now with the very personal pronoun, "will choose to do the same someday, when you can."

My knees were nearly giving way from standing motionless for so long, but this wasn't the sort of conversation you just walked away from. The practical part of my mind, the realist in me, told me (and maybe this was right) that he took me for a younger and more foolish man, that this was a sham job of a really professional order and I was lucky ("where do you get your ideas?") to be experiencing it, but it was really starting to get to me.

Something small and habitually silent deep within me was beginning to hum with possibility. The chances were remote, but what if the guy was for real? What if he could offer me just what he claimed? Would I be able to worry less about the rent? Even a little help could go a long way. I could eat, sleep and breathe a novel.

I checked myself. Even supposing he could offer such a thing, there were other, darker possibilities. Was he a pervert? Was this all just a way to lure me behind closed doors and have his way with me in rubber yellow dishwashing gloves?

Isaac did something like reading my mind then, and it made an impression, even if he waved his arms a little too dramatically. "I know what you're thinking," he said. "But it's not like that. I like girls. This would be a professional relationship. A way for me to patronize the arts from the ground up."

Now he took on a methodical tone I hadn't heard from him before. Like a tour guide going over the finer points. Or a manager explaining a job to a new hire. He said he would pay for an apartment in a decent neighborhood—comfortable and cared for, but not extravagant—and there would be a stipend for living expenses. The only condition was that I would be expected to bend all of my energies, as much of the days and nights as could reasonably be expected, toward the pursuit of my creative work. I would have to do exactly that thing—be it writing, music, whatever—that I'd always dreamed of doing. He knew people, powerful people in education, industry, publishing. He would get my work in front of them.

My eyes were wide. The afternoon was more than half-spent by this time. Little did I know that the bombs in his cargo bay were only half dropped.

When he'd talked about the accident, he'd worn an easy smile—the smile of a man who had come to terms with some difficult realities—and when he'd talked about the stipend, he'd been all business. But now his face darkened.

"When this happened to me," he made a gesture down his bent torso as if to say *look at what they did to me*, "I learned a lot about my family." He had no children of his own, but his siblings and their children had come on the run when they'd heard the news about his accident. He'd been in a medical coma, but he'd caught the basic gist of their talk: "When will the old buzzard die, so we can split up his money and go home?"

There was a tear on Isaac's cheek. He shook it off. "I would never have treated any one of them that way."

And then he was back to the all-business voice.

"Which is part of what this is about. I'm no spring chicken. I need an heir." If the new business partnership he was proposing was a successful one, he went on to say, I would be in consideration for selection as heir to his estate, which was currently estimated at *37 million dollars*.

"But one thing at a time," he said.

I heard him out that afternoon, through to the end. I lost track of time rather completely, and in those days before text messaging, there was no very effective way to let my girlfriend know that I was alright, that I would be late, that something unusual was happening ("omg"). So I waited for an opportunity to insinuate myself into his flow of words, and—as politely as I could—I bowed out.

He didn't turn suddenly and snap at me. He didn't lose an ounce of his domineering good humor. He said, "Of course, of course," that I needed to go and be with my people, but he hoped that I would consider what he'd said and would meet with him in a few days at the Hillman Library on the University of Pittsburgh's campus. He would have his lawyer draw up a contract for me in the meantime. I could check it out on Saturday.

Numb with wonder at the things I was hearing and good old-fashioned ("reasonable doubt") uncertainty, I agreed. I imagine there was a little stagger in my motion toward the escalator, past a row of cashiers and out the double doors. On the street, it felt like I was drawing my first breath since "Self Help."

At the restaurant, I found my girlfriend and my roommate caught up enough in conversation (and the beginnings of dinner) that my tardiness merited not much more than a passing comment. I hinted at what had happened to me, but I didn't really know how to talk about it without revealing the elicit little kernel of hope that had been planted in me. "I met the craziest guy," you know, and "he talked my head off." We moved on to talk of friends and work and the coming good weather.

I know one of the big reasons people don't dare to hope: they're afraid that when it comes out—molded in the exact shape of their dream, their secret passion—it will not measure up. No one wants to have such a thing out there and blinking in the sunlight for the first time, only to find it elicits ridicule. Worse even than ridicule is the very real possibility that the social situation will require you to join in the jeering yourself: "Yeah, I always wanted to be a musician.... I know. Might as well have wanted to be an astronaut. Pretty stupid, huh?"

For the next few days, I made the choice to move on. I did normal things. Worked a temp job. Hung out with friends. Kept myself carefully distracted. But when Saturday came, I put on my shoes and walked to Oakland without having made any conscious decision to do so. I'd give the crazy man one more say, and maybe see this mythical contract. I'd give my hope a glimpse of daylight and a little fresh air.

The Hillman Library was practically deserted. I hesitated at the door, wondering if as a non-student I was even welcome. Anyway, if Isaac was crazy, was it likely he kept appointments? How long would I be expected to wait, by myself, if he didn't? My mind raced through the possibilities.

It's a hidden camera show, I thought. There would be a big reveal and the consolation prize (sorry about your dream, buddy) would be 14 minutes of the degrading reality-TV-sort-of fame.

Screw it, I thought. *What do I have to lose?*

Isaac was waiting at the end of a long, lunch-room-style table in an otherwise empty side room, seated with a short stack of manila folders next to him like he was ready to review my credentials for a business interview.

I approached. Gave him a weak smile. Sat opposite him in a chair that felt like it had been built with some-one squarer and more substantial in mind.

Two things happened during that second meeting: (1) I realized that I'd "fallen down the rabbit hole" a bit during our last encounter, that he had a hypnotic way about him that could take away many hours of a person's life if they'd let him, and (2) knowledge of the fact rendered me more or less immune. I began to take the floor with greater frequency. In fact, after the ameni-ties were dispensed with, I informed him that my time was unfortunately limited and pushed the meeting as best I could toward its ostensible purpose, the contract.

"Oh, yes," he said. But the conversation, oddly, began to drift—and then slip—dramatically away from this subject.

I made another attempt. He fingered the edges of the topmost manila folder. He brought up Aristotle.

I took a level breath and asked him directly. "I'm very interested in taking a look at this contract. May I?" I gestured toward the folder.

This triggered a change in expression at last. Isaac went from amicable and easy to tight-lipped and guarded, and then he began making excuses.

He was "terribly sorry." It had been a hard time for his lawyer. They had not had time or opportunity to draw up the standard contract. Could we arrange to meet again next week?

I, of course, felt I'd called his bluff. Surely, I knew the truth now. There was never going to be a contract. There would only be more meetings, more of the hypnotic pulse of Isaac's talking. He'd done this. He's been there. He was going to help me. But nothing would ever materialize.

I'd made up my mind, and I didn't hear him anymore. I extricated myself on the friendliest possible terms, thanked him, smiled, told him I needed to think about it—that I'd consider a contract when he had one—and walked away with no intention of ever seeing him again, if I could help it.

As I set out for the single room that was serving me as an apartment, I decided I'd probably had a scrape with a harmless kind of kook—an old man desperate for talk. But how could I know for sure? The lack of proof one way or the other left me with a sort of Schrö-dinger's Cat situation, an odd little present in the back of my head that I could never hope to open.

By the time I made it home, I was surprised to find that my complex feelings on the subject had a consis-tent recurring feature: I was relieved. It might have been nice to have all the time in the world to work on a book, or write an album, or learn to paint, but I would always have felt the debt that was owed. From here on, I resolved, I would do what I would do and be what

I would be. I would use my own discretion and oper-
ate under my own power. For better or worse, I would
choose, and I would take the responsibility.

Not surprisingly, I found myself avoiding the bookstore in the months and years that followed. In my life,
I found ways to occupy myself, and some other ways
to make money, and most of the time I had no reason to
think about "the offer."

Once, I ran into Isaac, standing on the sidewalk
in Squirrel Hill. He was very happy to see me, asked
very specific questions about how things were going
for me. The old smile was there. He said he had always
respected me for "choosing not to take him up on his
offer." He said I was "obviously doing well" for myself.
This seemed to please him a great deal.

When I saw the first sparks of the old magic, I smiled
big. I told him it was great to see him and excused
myself with what was actually a valid explanation. I
crossed the street and made my way quickly down the
sidewalk, not looking back.

Maybe you'd like to stop here. Maybe that's all you
want to know. If so, thank you for your time. Nice to
see you. This is a good place to stop, if you've got the
choice.

Four years after my book-shop encounter with Isaac,
I brought home a copy of the *Pittsburgh City Paper*. My

girlfriend was now my fiancée, and the hope was to find interesting date options for the weekend. I threw the little rag on the bed. It popped open to a page somewhere near the middle.

There was Isaac looking up at me. The smile was gone. The man in the photo had flashed a dead ironic sort of look at the camera.

I was stunned. I sat down. But the article was not about Isaac. It was about the national database of sex offenders and the new Megan's Law website, designed to help protect the public—especially young girls with names like "Megan"—from such people. The clipping showing Isaac was just a sample from the site. Perhaps it had been chosen at random, but perhaps it had been chosen because the man in the photo and the attached copy were especially frightening, and especially unusual.

I was able to use the information from the clipping (full name, occupations, etc.) to find articles and notes from court cases online. The missing piece—my unopened present to myself—was opening up, and it was pretty dark down there.

Over a period of a decade, Isaac had engaged young men in conversation in public places, making promises of patronage. Promises of modest apartments in nice neighborhoods, no strings attached, if they would only get their lives into gear, if they would go out swinging into a life of creative work. He would introduce them to powerful people, captains of industry.

What in fact happened in at least three cases was that these young men would wind up living with Isaac in his apartment in a state of light servitude. "The doors were never locked," I read in a court report. The victims could have left at any time, but they didn't.

He kept them prisoner with the power of his speech and with the dark promises he made. He claimed, apparently, to have connection to a mob family. He told these unfortunate young souls that their families were in danger. He told one young man that he would kill his sister's daughter if he didn't do as he asked. These young men were made to perform sexual acts. One stole power tools from the building superintendent for Isaac. It would verge on the comical if it weren't so terrible. Isaac was a powerful personality.

The police and the local media used the word *Svengali*, and while I told myself (I tell myself) I was never in danger of coming fully under his sway, that I was simply along for the ride, lured by my writerly fascination with what a human being could say to another human being in the real world, isn't it probable that these other young men—these people whose only crime had been to dream—had thought exactly the same thing?

Enter the cliché: I have made lemonade. Whether Isaac was in any respect what he said he was (I've found no evidence of his career as a novelist, for instance), he was a man who created worlds so effectively with words, a person who could so vividly play on the human heartstrings—telling people precisely what they most wanted to hear—that his audiences were literally powerless to resist.

I won't soon forget this demonstration of what words can do, or the visceral reminder that such power is rendered terrible or glorious by the intentions of the wielder.

Um, thanks, Isaac.

 *Douglas Gwilym is a former background investigator, DJ, rock-n-roll singer and bassist, grant writer, graphic designer and academic. He and his wife live with their articulate and wild-haired toddler in America's most livable and historically peculiar city (Pittsburgh). He edits scholarly works for fun and profit under an assumed name, and has written many short stories and two novels of the darkly fantastic.*

MOTOR MEN

Scott Bradley Smith

MY DAD SOLD CARS FOR A LIVING. For more than 40 years, he'd take customers out on the lot and show them new Chevys, describe each of the various options, the interiors, the trim packages. If they liked what they saw, they bought it. If they didn't, my dad never pressed them. His style wasn't hard-sell, and his customers stayed with him for years, even sometimes when they moved away. We used to call him "the last honest car salesman in the world."

The Chevy dealership was in my hometown of Elizabethtown, a bedroom community halfway between Harrisburg and Lancaster, Pennsylvania. On the plywood walls of my dad's office hung framed certificates and wood plaques that he'd been awarded for sales leadership. For selling the most cars in sales contests, he won trips that he and my mom took all over the world—Hawaii, Jamaica, Nassau, England, France, Spain, Morocco—places they'd never imagined having the means to visit and where they felt almost embarrassed to be when they got there. He earned enough to pay the mortgage on our little brick ranch house, keep a second vehicle (a used, mint-green Chevy Suburban with an 8-track player) and buy a little silver and white travel trailer called a Mustang. When Dinah Shore sang the jingle "See the U.S.A. in Your Chevrolet," my dad took her literally. We were on the road a lot, and sometimes in less than ideal situations—downpours that made it hard to see the road, flat tires on busy expressways, strangers camping alongside us who partied too much or seemed like they might be criminals on the run. But I always felt secure knowing that my dad was behind the wheel, navigating us through traffic and out onto the open road.

My dad made me feel secure in other ways, too. When I was about seven, he helped to catch a voyeur in our neighborhood. It was after the nightly news, and I was already in bed. My dad always made sure the front door was locked before turning in, and as he did so that night, he took a peek out the little rectangle of a window. That's when he saw someone on the front porch of the Garmans' house across the street. The figure was leaning over the wrought-iron railing to try to peek in the bathroom window. My dad called the Garmans, and

Barry Garman said he would sneak out the back door and come around the house. He asked my dad to rush across the street at the same time. So, that's what they did. The voyeur was surprised and took off running. Barry and my dad chased him through a couple back-yards before they tackled him to the ground. Somehow, though, the guy broke loose and ran away.

I got up when my dad came home, and when he told us the story, I was thrilled by it. I suspected, even then, that Barry Garman—being younger and more athletic—had done most of the actual chasing and tackling, and that my dad had gone along mainly for moral support and got drawn into the struggle. But I could still picture every last detail of it. I could feel the damp chill of the ground as they rolled the guy around, the panic in his flailing, the desperation as he tore away from them and ran, ran for his life. It was too bad the guy got away, but I nevertheless felt safe knowing that my dad could help defend our home, his family and his neighbors when he needed to. He was as much a hero as anyone could be to me then.

A Saturday night in the summer of 1969 changed all that. We were headed home from delivering a new car to one of my dad's customers near Selinsgrove, along the Susquehanna River. I was eight, maybe nine. George Gutshall, another salesman from my dad's dealership, rode shotgun up front, an arm across the top of the seat. He smoked a cigarette, flicking the ashes from the vent window with his beefy hand. George had driven the new car to the customer, and we had followed to bring him home. My mom and my younger sister nodded off beside me in the back seat of our latest demonstrator, likely a Caprice Classic. My dad got a new car to drive about every six months, always a boxy four-door sedan with bench seats. I assumed everyone's car smelled like fresh vinyl all the time.

George was about ten years younger than my dad, unmarried, big in every way but up. When he dipped his crew-cut head to look down at me, his chin folded into multiples of itself. He was thick-necked and barrel-chested, and he wore the sleeves of his white work shirts rolled to display a pair of the most powerful forearms I'd ever seen. He was also profoundly jolly, yakking constantly, making cracks that my dad laughed along with—all this in a high-pitched voice that never seemed like it belonged to him. He was the kind of adult who could relate to kids, always kneeling down and asking my sister and me what was new at school or buying us a bottle of Coke from the mechanics' vending machine in the garage.

That night, as we came down Front Street in Harrisburg, the traffic was surprisingly light for a weekend night. Back then, I believed Harrisburg was a dangerous place—full of poor people, most of whom were black—where, if I were to trust the evening news, serious crimes were committed at an alarming rate. When driving through certain parts of the city, my parents instructed us to crank up our windows and lock our doors. That night, with the air conditioning on and the windows up, we came to a stop at a red light behind a sleek black Corvette. Over George's arm, I could just see the flat snub of the Corvette's back end, the four round taillights. I built model cars from kits, and the two Corvettes I'd put together were my favorites so far.

While the Corvette waited there, a woman leaned into the window to talk to the driver and another guy in the passenger seat. I figured it was just somebody they knew. When the light turned green, the guys in the Corvette and their friend kept right on talking. The light changed to red again. My dad laid on the horn.

Understand that my dad was never the most patient driver. Cars were his living, so he assumed a moral and technical superiority over most other drivers. Combine this with his half-German, half-English ancestry and you got a driver who followed the rules of the road almost to a tee and expected everyone else to do the same. Now, it was important for my dad to make a statement, to point out the other driver's fallibility, his clear and utter lack of consideration for the cars behind him. When the light finally did change to green again, my dad flicked his high beams on and off. Then, horn blaring, he squealed a tight arc around the Corvette and sped away.

Apparently, the driver of the Corvette had similar ideas. As I turned around and kneeled on the seat—

which was easy to do, since we weren't wearing seat belts (almost no one did then)—the Corvette roared up behind us, the headlights closing in on our bumper. The hood of the car reflected each street light in a glowing zip. The heads of the guys inside were silhouettes.

At first, I was oddly thrilled by this aggression. It felt like I was in the midst of a car chase on *Hawaii Five-O*, my favorite TV show. I bounced up and down on the seat. At the next light, the Corvette growled—a sound I could feel through the upholstery—and crept within inches of our bumper. It was so close that I could no longer see its headlights. I smiled a friendly smile, wondering if the driver and his passenger could see me. But when the light turned green, the Corvette whipped around us, pulled in front and slowed to a crawl, forcing my dad to brake, and brake again. The high-speed chase had switched to a low-speed game of stop and go.

By now, my dad had become irate. I could see only a slice of his face when he jerked his head to look in the rear-view mirror. His cheek was taut, jaw set in a rigid line. He wrenched the wheel from side to side. In the backseat, my mom had been roused and began trying to simmer him down. "Dale, stop it," she said, leaning between the head rests. "You're scaring the kids."

But my mom's words of warning seemed to provoke my dad even more. He pulled into the passing lane and drag-raced the Corvette to the next light, as George Gutshall merely grunted and held on, one arm bulged against the door. My mom upped her harangue: "Stop it, Dale! Stop it right now!" Her voice had taken on a sharpness I'd rarely heard from her. My sister started mimicking my mom's insistence: "Stop it! Slow down!" Now I really *did* begin to feel afraid, a raw fear I felt in my chest and in my belly.

When my dad jumped the green and veered in front, sped up for most of a block, the Corvette stayed right on our tail. I peered out the back window and bobbed my head, hoping the driver of the Corvette would see me and realize there were innocent kids onboard. Maybe that would make him back off. But then, as the light up ahead turned yellow, my dad slammed on the brakes.

The crunch of steel on steel is a sound like no other—a ragged groaning that seems more reptilian and monsterly than the inanimate metal it really is. The Corvette hit us with a force that lifted our car in the air and pummeled us partway into the intersection. I rammed the seat ahead of me and was thrown back again. There was an aftershock of hissing water and tinkling glass, and the collective gasps of everyone inside our car.

I scrambled to turn around and look out the back. The Corvette had submarined us, half its hood underneath our bumper. Instantly, it seemed, the Corvette guy was out of his car and sneering in at my dad's window. Even as my mom was checking to make sure my sister and I weren't hurt, the guy began beating on the glass with clenched fists, his face red and twisted in rage. "You son-of-a-bitch," he screamed. "Open up, goddamn it. Get out of the car!" From where I sat, I could see that the guy was younger than my dad, tall and wiry. He wore a sport jacket over a black t-shirt. The sinews of his neck tautened as he clenched his teeth and spat invective at my dad's window.

My dad sat there, contemplating. Driving habits aside, he'd usually been more interested in keeping the peace than in instigating conflict. Not long after World War II, he'd joined the Navy and was stationed in Panama where he worked as a radio operator. Occasionally he'd pull shore duty as master-at-arms, which meant that he had to go into town and break up fights and yank drunken sailors out of what he called "cat houses." He didn't seem to enjoy this part of his service life and never talked about being in any fights of his own. Then there was my dad's physique. He was stocky, his height skewing to the short side. He wasn't made for grappling and punching and drawing blood.

So, as the Corvette guy beat on the window, my dad stared straight ahead like he couldn't even hear the pounding just inches from his left earlobe. "Don't you open that door," said my mom in as firm a voice as she could muster.

Some other cars came by, giving us a wide berth. Eventually, my dad turned to the window, shrugged. "Hey, you shouldn't have been following me so close," he said through the glass.

The Corvette guy shook his fists in the air, then disappeared for a moment to the back of our car—presumably to survey the damage. The other guy was getting out of the Corvette now, too, stretching his long legs in the street. I perched forward on the seat. I no longer felt thrilled, no longer craved the unexpected turn of events. What if one of them had a knife? Or a gun? What if they shot and killed the entire carload of us? The driver's anger seemed to have no bounds; no lock or window could resist it for very long. Please, dear God, I thought. Please just let this be over with. Please, don't let us all die. I felt short of breath, the blood pounding in my temples like tiny knuckles.

The driver came back to my dad's window, started beating the glass again. "Get out of the goddamned car!"

My dad turned to George Gutshall and said, "I don't know why he's so upset. Everyone knows it's the guy in back's fault in a rear-ender."

George shrugged, uncharacteristically quiet, the cigarette now burning down to his fingers.

To my dismay, my dad got out of the car, taking his time to shut the door behind him. Right away, the Corvette guy pushed his chest into my dad and started chewing him out. I was sure the guy was about to beat my dad to a pulp, and then do who knew what to the rest of us. Shouldn't my dad start throwing punches? Wasn't he going to defend himself? He looked small and weak then, older too. I wondered if I should jump out and help him, that together maybe we could over-whelm the guy. But all I did was gawk out the window and hope the guy might see me and take pity.

"Dale!" my mom yelled. "Dale!" Then she slumped back in the seat. "Why can't he listen?" she said to no one in particular.

That's when George Gutshall opened the passenger door and grunted his way out onto the street. He tossed away his cigarette. Then he flexed his arms and came around the front of our car, sweeping his hand over the hood. George pushed my dad aside and stood right up in the Corvette guy's face, said something in his high-pitched voice that sounded like, "Calm down, buddy. Just calm the heck down." The guy saw George's biceps, the solid bulk, the curled fists that resembled baby hams, and his demeanor changed at once. He held up his hands and backed off.

Now, the driver pointed at his car, began to sputter what sounded like an explanation of why his outburst was justified. George crossed his arms and listened, his head moving in chopped, jowly nods. My dad stood off to the side with the Corvette guy's passenger. They seemed to be merely onlookers who had stumbled upon the scene. George yakked at the guy a bit more, no doubt making him see the errors of his ways. The Corvette guy began to look sheepish, almost apologetic.

Sitting there in the safety of the back seat with my mom and my sister, I began to understand what it meant to have a real-life hero swoop in and save the day. I wanted to roll down my window and cheer for George. But then a cop showed up and ushered all four men to the curb where he began to take statements. As the blue and red lights of the police cruiser bounced around the interior, I began to wonder what would happen if they hauled my dad away to jail. Fortunately, George was a volunteer fireman who also knew how to talk to cops. He had the cop joking around in no time, and soon a wrecker was pulling up to tow the Corvette away, and George and my dad crossed back to our car and got in.

Our car was, fortunately, drivable, and we started off again, moving on through the dark city. No one spoke. At home that night, once I was in bed, I could hear my mom upbraiding my dad in the next room. Though I couldn't understand her words, I knew that she was scolding him for putting us all at risk, telling him it had better not happen again. Never one to give in easily, my dad argued back a bit, but eventually conceded. After all, he really didn't have much to stand on, did he? As the house grew quiet, the knocking in my temples subsided and the universe seemed to find its balance again. But it was a different kind of balance than before, one in which the pivot point had moved and come to rest in a strange and different place.

From that day forward, whenever I visited the dealership and George Gutshall gripped his massive hand in mine, whether in greeting or in congratulations for some school achievement, I thought of the day he'd saved my dad, and possibly all of us, from certain harm. He hadn't thrown a punch, hadn't cursed. He'd just approached the scene with unbridled confidence, flashing muscles and yapping away, making a statement with a body he'd maybe wished, most of the time, wasn't so large.

But for all the respect George had gained in my estimation, it had come at a price. I no longer believed my dad could always keep me safe. From now on, if I wanted to avoid collisions on the road ahead, I was going to have to take my own evasive measures—staying vigilant and steering clear of danger when I saw it. And if the collisions weren't avoidable? Well, I was going to have to figure out how to summon my own courage and meet them head on, preferably the way George had done. With candor and confidence and strength.

My dad retired from selling cars in 1995 at age 65 and lived ten more years. George Gutshall passed away just last year, at age 72. Recently I was recalling the story of the car crash with one of my aunts, who had worked as a bookkeeper at the same dealership. She waited until I finished before saying, "He was a peeping tom, you know."

"George Gutshall?"

"That was the rumor. One time, I heard a sound outside. I just opened the front door and yelled out, 'George Gutshall, you go home!' I guess he did."

So George had his vices too, crass imperfections that made my dad's—and by association mine—seem normal by comparison. I remembered the voyeur my dad and Barry Garman had chased down in our neighborhood when I was a kid. Could it have been George Gutshall peering in the Garmans' bathroom window? Could it be that, when they tackled him, my dad realized who it was and convinced Barry to let him go? Was it possible that, years before the car crash, my dad had actually saved George from embarrassment and a criminal record?

Whatever the story, I picture them now, in their own personal heavens, cruising around together in a four-door family sedan, trying to keep each other out of certain trouble, cracking jokes that make them slap the flesh of their bellies and laugh, all the way to the pearly garage doors, and beyond.

&

Scott Bradley Smith *has been gain-fully employed as a produce peddler, box boy, bus boy, bowling alley cleaner, electronics parts assembler, waiter, university instructor, legal document coder, public relations specialist, communications generalist and freelance writer. He left Tucson, Arizona in the early '90s to run a writers commune in Pittsburgh, which spawned a hefty body of work and at least one baby. He plays bass in an improvisational band that doesn't yet have the nerve to play out. For more on Scott, visit www.scottbradleysmith.com.*

MENTOR IN THE DARK

Laura Lind

I'M NOT SURE WHETHER TAMAR KNEW I was a little afraid of her. On the surface, it would have seemed ridiculous. She was petite—several inches shorter than I, and only two years older. Yet she had a worldliness about her and had experiences that seemed unreal to me. She could also be as tough as any teacher I ever had.

I met Tamar at Carnegie Mellon University (CMU) in Scotch'n'Soda, the student-run drama organization. I initially joined Scotch'n'Soda as a member of its writing workshop, during which the group members mentioned the acting workshops enough times that it piqued my interest. I had always been drawn to theater, but had no great experience aside from a few bumbling school productions and some backyard creations with the other neighborhood kids. Tamar, on the other hand, had been a drama major who had left college for a year-long break after she was a freshman and performed improvisational comedy in New York City. So, around the time I was plodding my way through my brief appearance as a Western Union telegraph operator in a faltering rendition of *Sorry, Wrong Number* in high school, Tamar was entertaining the public in New York. She was performing for people who had actually paid to see her. People who weren't her parents or relatives of classmates.

Though I love theater, I am not the type of person most people would think of as a "theater person." To this day, I am reserved—shy at times—and soft-spoken. These qualities were even more pronounced in college. I was never cutting-edge in my actions or appearance. I wore jeans and colorful t-shirts with pictures or words on them—like Snoopy or our school's logo shirts. I had never lived anywhere but Pittsburgh. I preferred to listen to mainstream pop on the radio, with a strong leaning toward oldies from the '50s and '60s. Tamar, on the other hand, always wore all black, usually a long black skirt and long-sleeved black shirt. She had lived in other, bigger cities and knew about alternative bands that weren't on my radar at all. I was the little college kid. She was the artiste behind a mysterious swirl of cigarette smoke. And, unlike me, she wasn't afraid to speak up, which is how she taught me to be a performer.

When I was a child, my father created improvised man-on-the-street interviews with me on cassette tapes.

This became a favorite activity for me and my friends. My elementary school friends and I made cassette recordings of our original versions of fairy tales like *Little Red Riding Hood*. In high school, my friend Elinor and I spent many Saturday evenings creating and acting out made-up episodes of *Fantasy Island, The Love Boat* and *The Brady Bunch*. I loved concocting these stories, but I never saw them as improvising—just playing and having fun. And they entertained only us, the two creators, not a group.

So, I had to scrape my shreds of courage together to attend the acting workshops. I was a writing major, not an acting major, and it seemed like such a serious step. It wasn't just goofing around in my living room. In these workshops, the other students and I performed skits for each other with no script. We were supposed to create everything—faceted characters, engaging plots, invisible scenery—beneath unforgiving fluorescent lights in a meeting room in the student union. It was exposing. Being surrounded by talented, seemingly fearless fellow students was intimidating. Being under the scrutiny of a mentor who focused her attention on every move we made and every word we uttered was daunting. However, it was also an amazing, limitless, creative new world. Tamar taught us a variety of improv games, many that helped catapult us into scenes of absurd comedy, but also several with a dramatic bent. This was way before Drew Carey's improv show, *Whose*

Line Is It Anyway?, appeared on American TV. At that time, in the late '80s, these games were avant-garde.

Workshops were fun and often hilarious. I delighted in watching the others create ridiculous scenarios. In one of the earliest scenes I remember, two guys took a beating heart out of someone and made a pizza with it. Where else could I see a scene like that? Their ingenuity and quick senses of humor impressed me. How did they think so quickly? How could they be so funny so easily?

As entertaining as the workshops were, they were also challenging. Tamar often stopped us in the middle of a scene to change a choice we had made that wasn't working. If we were standing still and talking too much (what Tamar called "talking heads"), she would stop the scene and tell us to continue it with no words, thus forcing us to move around the performance space. As we worked through each scene, Tamar would scribble plentiful notes on the clipboard she always carried. At the end of a scene, she would reveal to us what had worked and what hadn't. In these early days of the improv workshops, I could barely speak and, when I did, my voice was thin and hesitant. Tamar continually told me to speak in a louder voice, a note I got so often she probably had it permanently etched into the paper next to my name. It could be difficult to hear critiques that weren't favorable, but the more I heard focused comments on my work and that of the others, the more I absorbed. I learned from the positive feedback as well.

When I received it, it made me feel excited that even shy, quiet Laura had something to offer.

I remember being so nervous about having to improvise a monologue in an early workshop. I infused my real-life anxiety into a character with a speech impediment and talked about how holding onto a special trinket helped me get through difficulties in school. I worried that my monologue was terrible. When I finished, Tamar said, "Laura, that was beautiful. It was so moving." I still remember the jolt of shocked pride I felt as I realized that, like the character I had just invented, I was becoming more able to express myself.

After learning improv for several months, Tamar decided that our big spring show would be all-improv. This was a gutsy move, especially since the drama organization was floundering, trying to recover from an abysmal show the previous spring. My college "Acting for Non-Majors" teacher said an improv show would never work. Some students in the improv workshops doubted the show's potential success and bowed out before rehearsals commenced.

Tamar was not dissuaded. She put us through a rigorous rehearsal process, giving the pen and clipboard an even greater workout than usual. She not only critiqued our choices while we played the improv games, but also turned a detailed eye toward our stage presence and our professionalism. If we stood with our hands clasped in front of ourselves while standing neutrally on stage, she told us we looked indecent. "You look like you're holding yourselves!" she'd yell. Whenever Tamar gave us this note, I imagined us as scrawny, insecure Adams and Eves, trying to cover ourselves without the aid of fig leaves. We learned to clasp our hands behind our backs. She absolutely never wanted to see us peeking from behind the curtains during the show to see who was in the audience. That behavior, she told us, was amateurish and unacceptable.

As opening night approached, we all got queasy, wondering if we were capable enough to entertain people other than ourselves. Just when our nerves had been stretched to hair-trigger sensitivity, Tamar tripled her toughness factor. A few days before opening night, her frustration and fury at our sloppiness pelted us in a "motivational" speech I've never forgotten.

"I'll be sitting in the dark in the back of the theater!" she growled. "Nobody will know who *I* am. It's *you* who'll be making fools of yourselves up there!" She flung her clipboard onto the floor and stormed away.

What if we do *get up there and flop?* I wondered. *What if the audience is dead-silent?* Or worse yet, *What if they walk out?*

Tamar's pep talk worked, though. The improv show was so successful that we had to add another to accommodate the audience demand. We performed five shows in four days. It was an incredible experience. Most of the audience had never seen an improvised show, and we as performers had never dreamed of the delighted whoops and applause we received.

Although we were thrilled with our accomplishments, we were not allowed to scream with glee and congratulate ourselves backstage when the show was over. We had to wait several minutes before coming out to greet the audience. To run out immediately smacked of a high-school production, Tamar had warned us. I had never thought about such details but realized she was right. When I went to see professional theater productions, the actors never squealed backstage or rushed out in their costumes before the final curtain had settled back into place.

After our spring show, I knew I was hooked. Tamar had given me the opportunity to experience pure joy and camaraderie, as well as the chance to discover aspects of myself I hadn't previously known. I wanted to continue performing improv, and I was willing to deal with Tamar's uncompromising drive to do that.

Shortly after I graduated from college, Tamar and another classmate of mine, Jessie, formed a theater company called Flying Pig Theatre and wanted to get it off the ground by launching an improvisational comedy troupe. They gathered those of us who had improvised together and had remained in Pittsburgh—some of whom were still students at CMU. We called our troupe

Reality Optional and began twice-weekly rehearsals, most of which took place in the college classrooms where I had recently studied.

While I knew by that point that improv shows could be successful, the stakes were higher. This time, we were attempting what Tamar had done several years previously—to perform for the general public. Our venue was The Artery, a restaurant/bar on Ellsworth Street in Shadyside, an area that was only beginning to revitalize itself from a shabby state of inertia. There, on a small, foot-high stage in the shadow of bar patrons, we hoped to get the same response we received in college. Or at least not get booed out of the place.

During one rehearsal, Tamar was annoyed at our comedic choices. In an effort to show us how unusual, unique ideas could be hilarious, she put a foil muffin baking cup on her head. *"This* is comedy!" she fumed, thrusting her index finger toward the cup. As we stared at her, the wrinkled aluminum cup balanced in her black hair, we painfully feigned seriousness to keep from exploding with laughter—not because a muffin baking cup on a head was inherently funny, but because the situation was so ridiculous. Actually, a furious woman with a muffin baking cup on her head *was* pretty funny, but we all knew better than to acknowledge that at the time.

As harsh as Tamar's critiques could be, I always believed that she cared about us and about the product she was trying to create—a successful performance. She truly enjoyed much of what we did. Just as she wasn't reserved in telling us what we could improve, she never hesitated to tell us what we did well. One of the greatest compliments I felt I could get was to hear Tamar's jovial guffaw as I worked in a scene. She seemed to take great pleasure in watching us grow in our work, and shared our delight when scenes took hilarious turns. She often seemed to be creating right along with us, and was so absorbed in the stories we created that she went into a bit of a trance at times. As she would watch our scenes, she would usually mouth the words along with us as we talked, as if it were a scripted show. Her lips would move with each word, interrupted sporadically with hearty laughs. Someone once pointed this out, and Tamar laughed in acknowledgment. Then she mouthed along with the next scene.

Tamar's methods worked again. Reality Optional's first show at The Artery was packed to capacity, thanks to the promise of an innovative show with considerable advance PR via the newspapers and posters that were hung around the city. We weren't booed out of the club but, rather, received a warm, enthusiastic response—and lots of laughs. We performed twice a month for nearly five years at The Artery, as well as at other local clubs, colleges and private parties. Though these experiences were generally positive, we did have to face drunk audience members, people ignoring us in a roar of conversation during our shows and, yes, people walking out on us. It happens. But because of the training I'd had with Tamar, I could survive—and even laugh at—some of these more difficult times. Overall, the improv group was a successful, enjoyable endeavor.

Reality Optional never had an official final performance. We took a little break from performing improv shows and never resumed. People moved on and moved away, and I lost touch with Tamar. However, she'd planted a love of improv in me that still wasn't satisfied.

For more than fourteen years now, I have been a member of The Amish Monkeys, an improvisational comedy group I helped found, performing with some of the same people from my days under Tamar's leadership. Hundreds of performances in various venues have certainly taught me plenty, but I know that it was the foundation with Tamar that enabled me to be a performer. Her insistence on professionalism has been my guidance during the many shows I've done. I like to believe I wouldn't get the "speak up" note from Tamar today.

It has always been important to me that The Amish Monkeys represent ourselves professionally. Other members of the troupe wilt and sigh when I close the door to the cramped dressing room where we warm up backstage before the show. I don't want the audience to hear us joking around and making silly noises as we get ready for the performance. The dressing room can get quite warm, with eight bodies in a tight circle, but I would rather sweat a bit than have the audience hear us. I know that Tamar instilled this fussiness in me.

I try to maintain an eager, energetic stage presence, even when I don't feel that way. I've performed both when I've been sick and to audiences who've ignored us (which is very difficult in a show where you rely on audience interaction). I've learned to plow through and keep smiling, because the audience didn't pay to see me give a half-hearted effort. That's what being a professional means. That's what Tamar taught me all those years ago in a musty college meeting room.

And anytime I catch myself standing neutrally onstage with my hands clasped in front of me, I think of Tamar and quickly whisk them behind me.

There are few people that I can say truly changed the course of my life. Tamar is one such person. Without having met her, I still might have learned about improv and played some improv games, but not many people— college students, no less—could have given me the opportunity and the knowledge to perform professionally.

I realize, now, that Tamar had been right. No one really did know who she was, sitting in the back of the dark theater—or club or restaurant. While she didn't have to endure the immediate, unrelenting stress of being onstage, she also didn't get the direct acknowledgment she deserved. I hope to be able someday to tell her what I've learned from her. And I hope that, in the backs of those dark performance spaces, she privately accepted some of the applause for herself.

Laura Lind, *a lifelong Pittsburgher, enjoys creative pursuits in the arts, from dancing to jewelry making (although tiny beads and tangled wire tax her sanity). She has spent nearly her entire adult life performing in improv comedy groups. She finds improv more rewarding than scary—but still scary enough that if she really thought about it, she'd never get back onstage. Laura is a founding member of the improv comedy group The Amish Monkeys (www.amishmonkeys.com). She is also an early-childhood music teacher and a writer. In addition to writing plays and personal essays, Laura writes to promote animal adoptions, most recently for Steel City Greyhounds.*

ACCOUNTS RECEIVABLE

Anita Kulina

THE SMELL IS ALWAYS WHAT I REMEMBER FIRST. That sickly sweet, acrid smell.

I was, I don't know, probably nineteen. Maybe twenty. I'd been working there for close to a year. I typed purchase orders, though mostly what I did some days was run errands for the lady who worked at the other desk. She kept the books. Enormous volumes, almost a foot thick. They were stored in a cabinet by the front door. One of my jobs was to carry them back and forth to her desk.

There were two big books. Accounts Receivable, Accounts Payable. She wrote in them with a fountain pen, little numbers in blue or black. Adding and subtracting in her head. Checking the numbers at the end of the month with the clackety-clack of an adding machine. Waves of long white paper would spill out onto the floor. She would gather it all when she was done, fold it up in a neat little stack and put a rubber band around it.

In the back was a warehouse of sorts. Plumbing fixtures. Male and female parts. I was sometimes embarrassed to type the purchase orders because they sounded oddly sexual.

A guy my age worked in the back. I forget his name. He worked for an older guy who was in charge, a meek, quiet fellow. Polite. Probably about a year from retirement age, if that. There were a couple of salesmen, too. I don't really remember them. One's name was Joe, I do remember that.

The boss stopped in once in a while. He was a tall guy, and he had that lanky, lazy walk tall people sometimes have. He wore suits all the time, dark suits, and flashy ties. He was loud. Even as young and naïve as I was, I could tell he thought a lot of himself.

The older man and the bookkeeper always made a big fuss when the boss came in. The boss would talk to the older man about the Boca Raton orders. The enormous Accounts Receivable book had a page for each account. There were only a few in Boca Raton but they were big accounts. Apartment buildings, hotels. One of them was named Flamingo something. When I typed those purchase orders, they always included a bonus for the guy who bought the stuff, the purchasing agent. A color television, usually. Sometimes a stereo or a refrigerator, but always something big.

It was a quiet job, and I could walk there from my little apartment around the corner. Nobody talked to me all day, and there really wasn't enough for me to do. There wasn't enough for the bookkeeper to do, either. The two of us spent lots of days reading paperback books. She taught me how to read a book at my desk. You stick it in an open drawer and read it like that. Then, if the boss comes in, you shut the drawer and no one's been the wiser.

Most days were like that. Reading books. Occasionally I'd type purchase orders. Or run up the street to the supermarket for the bookkeeper. She always had me buy Zesta crackers and smoked oysters. She said that was her favorite dinner. She was an older lady, fifties at least, with jet-black hair. She was married, but I guess she didn't cook.

Her husband used to work there. I heard that from the older guy who worked in the back. The husband quit because he had a fight with the boss. He still couldn't understand why his wife continued to work there. She drove all the way in from Irwin or someplace like that. We were on the opposite side of the city. I bet it took her an hour to get there.

The boss wasn't there much. I hardly ever saw him. He spent a lot of time in Florida. The company was his father's baby. Everybody loved his father, I was told. But when the father died and the son took over, everything was different. That's when the bookkeeper's husband quit.

I never knew the father. I barely knew the son, the new boss. He'd call once in a while from Florida, and the bookkeeper would ask me to bring the giant Accounts Payable book over to her desk. They'd talk about it over the phone in hushed tones. We usually knew ahead of time when the boss was coming to the office. I'd be told to look like I was working. My back was to the door, but I would hear him come in. He never said anything to me. I don't think he knew my name.

That day, to me, started out the same as any other day working there. I came in, said good morning to the bookkeeper. Stuck my purse in my bottom drawer. I typed a purchase order or two on the IBM Selectric typewriter in the center of my desk. I put them in the in-box on the bookkeeper's desk. She'd have to sign them before they went out. They were three-part forms: white, yellow and pink. Carbon paper between, and all stuck together at the top where you put it into the type-writer. So you didn't get carbon on your hands.

I really liked that IBM Selectric. That was one of the best parts of the job. That, and they let me wear jeans.

Late morning, I think it was, the phone rang. The phone was on the bookkeeper's desk. The boss was on his way in. I tried to look busy, like I was told. I can't remember how. Probably put a stack of pink purchase-order copies on my desk and alphabetized them.

The boss burst through the door, like he always did. He was a little louder than usual and went straight to the back, where the older guy was. He talked to him for maybe a couple of minutes. I couldn't see them too well from where I was, but the older guy looked agitated. Then the boss announced he was going down to the basement. We were on the first floor of a three-story building, with apartments upstairs. I didn't even know we had a basement.

The older guy came out and started whispering to the bookkeeper. Her face turned to ash. She looked at me with these really big eyes, and then looked back and whispered with the older guy some more. I don't think anybody else was there that day. Just me, the bookkeeper and the older guy. And the boss, in the basement.

I didn't pay much attention to them after a while. Older people were still a mystery to me. I could never figure them out, and I wasn't interested enough to try. I fussed around at my desk and tried to look busy, like I was told. Since the boss was in the basement, every once in a while I'd get bored and sneak a look at the book in my desk drawer.

The older guy eventually went back to his desk. He was usually such a mellow guy but today he was completely shook up. He could hardly sit still on the tall wooden stool behind his desk. He kept looking at the bookkeeper. She would look at me sometimes, and she would look at him a lot. Her eyes were still big. She started to seem agitated, too.

Then the boss came up from the basement. There was smoke in the back room. By now the older guy looked like he would come apart at the seams. The boss came through our office and went straight out the front door. The older guy followed him.

The bookkeeper grabbed her purse and told me we were leaving. She asked me for the Accounts Receivable volume, in the cabinet on the other side of my desk. I tried to give her both of those giant books, but she said sharply, "No. Just Accounts Receivable."

She told me to get my purse and follow her out the door. She pointed to the little framed photo I had on my desk, I don't remember what it was, probably my boyfriend's senior picture. She told me to bring that, too. "Take anything that belongs to you," she said. "The building is on fire."

We went outside and stood on the sidewalk. I guess it was around lunchtime then, maybe a little after. I don't remember anyone calling the fire department while we were in there, but I guess eventually somebody did. The fire truck came and we had to move across the street. We just stood there and watched. I didn't know what else to do. By now there were flames.

A couple of the firemen went into the building through the back and went up to the apartments above.

An old woman lived on the second floor, and an old man lived on the third floor. They got them both out in time.

There was a bank on the corner, maybe three doors away. Some of the tellers came out to watch the fire. By now people from the butcher shop and the bakery were outside, too, watching. People were coming from a block away. The flames were really big now, and there was more than one fire truck.

The boss went into the bank and came out with a fistful of hundred-dollar bills.

That was when the smell started. That sickly, acrid smell. Burning building. I'd never smelled it before. I hope I never have to again.

We spent the whole afternoon out on the sidewalk. The tellers invited us into the bank for a little while, to sit down and have something to eat. They had a little kitchen in there. They made us chipped ham sandwiches. The rest of the time we stood on the sidewalk and watched the building burn to the ground.

It took a long time. There was a big crowd by the end of the afternoon. The firemen kept us pretty far away. There were flames for a while. Sparks flew sometimes, and big pieces of ash floated out over the street. Sometimes you'd hear a crash, or a boom. Pieces of the building collapsing.

I don't know what happened to the old people who lived upstairs. All their stuff was gone. The lady might have been crying. The man looked really old. He didn't look like he could walk all the way up to the third floor.

Toward the end of the day, the boss walked through the throng of firemen. He was all smiles and handshakes. He shook each fireman's hand and gave him some of the hundred-dollar bills. One of the firemen told me what a great guy my boss was.

I walked over to the building after it was all done. There was still a framework around most of the first floor and part of the second. I looked in. My beautiful IBM Selectric had melted into what was left of my desk. I didn't know metal could melt. I figured the fire must have been really, really hot.

There was a write-up in the paper the next week about our company. About how wonderful our boss was, keeping the company intact, the four of us working in a little motel room at the Howard Johnson's. I only worked there a couple of days. There wasn't really any way you could work in there. All we had was that Accounts Receivable book and a couple other things rescued from the fire. The bookkeeper was on the phone a lot. Everything in the motel room had that sickly, acrid, burning-building smell.

~

*Like most people who love to write, **Anita Kulina** has been telling stories since she was old enough to hold a pen. Her first publication was in the letters-to-the-editor column of* Adventure Comics #341. *Nowadays, much of her work centers around the rich and colorful lives of Pittsburgh's working poor. Since she spent much of her life in those ranks, it's a subject dear to her heart.*

DON'T BE STUPID

Seth Roskos

"FLIGHT 1690 TO HARRISBURG WILL BEGIN boarding in ten minutes," comes the voice over the PA. It's a Friday afternoon in May and I'm flying in for my brother Steven's wedding. I'm poring over a journal entry from earlier in the week, trying to come up with a theme for the toast I'll be expected to give. When not brainstorming methods to overcome my terror at the mere thought of a public address, I've been rifling through memories of all the good—and not so good—times we had as kids.

The first Halloween I remember I was six or seven, which makes Steven nine or ten. Probably the first time we'd been allowed to go trick-or-treating without an adult. It was the seventies. A safe neighborhood.

"Let's go to Pembroke first," my brother said, leading me down the center of Cascade Court, our shadows stretching dimly toward the curb on either side.

"Does Pembroke have good candy?" I asked.

"Probably an apple with a razor blade in it."

With the exception of the red Eveready flashlight my brother kept trained on the road before us, the only light streamed from the yellow windows in the split-level ranches and boxy colonials on either side.

"I don't want any apples," I said.

I wore a suit of red pajamas that my mother had drawn black spiderwebs across.

"Me either," my brother said in his best robot voice.

I laughed. He wore a silver box with three colored dots pasted on the front that looked something like the lights you might see on the front of a robot.

"Are you R2-D2?" We had waited in a line around the block to see *Star Wars* a few months before and it was still all I could think about.

"No."

"C-3PO?"

"I'm just a robot."

"I'm Spiderman."

"I know."

There were only nine houses on our cul-de-sac and we had yet to see a single car. We rounded the bend toward the bottom of the road where there were no houses, just a meadow gone to seed on one side and a sparse wood across the street. There was no moon, and the darkness would have been complete except for the distant window of an ominous colonial above the meadow and the beam of the flashlight, which turned everything outside its range blacker.

"What's that?" my brother said.

"What's what?"

"Shh." We both froze as the beam of the flashlight swung toward the woods. I heard leaves crunching as my brother tried to illuminate the source of the noise. He stepped between me and the sound, shoving me behind him with his free hand. But I stepped away and stood beside him.

"Cut it out," he said.

"I'm Spiderman," I replied.

When the scraping of my feet against the asphalt ceased, I could hear my brother's breath. Or was it mine? Then it stopped. Only the twisted gray branches snaked through the disk of light scanning the woods. Leaves crunched in the darkness again. The disk of light jerked toward the sound. The crunching quickened into shuffling, then rushing. A pair of silhouettes burst from the edge of the woods and were upon us. My brother and I fell back, the beam of the flashlight shooting skyward. Sssssshhhhhhhhhhhhh. The hiss of aerosol filled our ears as two white streams shot toward us from the hands of the figures.

We hit the asphalt as the figures danced around us, screaming and laughing maniacally, crisscrossing our backs with thin white lines of shaving cream. As we realized the danger was only to our pride and clambered to our feet, the figures slipped down the street toward the larger road.

"Who was that?" I said, gaping as the figures rounded the corner and faded into darkness. I could feel my lower lip trembling while the soapy-clean smell filled my nostrils.

"Teenagers," my brother said, as if the word itself were an insult.

He stepped behind me and brushed the shaving cream off my back as well as he could.

"I want to go home," I said, struggling not to sob.

"And tell Mom and Dad?"

I contemplated. This wasn't the type of thing we would tell our parents. Dad would head out to troll the streets in his gold Granada looking for the hooligans, and Mom would be calling parents to try and locate them.

"I wanna beat those guys up," I said. A tear escaped from my eyelid, a knot twisted in the pit of my stomach.

"They're teenagers."

"I don't care."

"They'd kill us." He turned his back to me. "Get the shaving cream off me."

"I don't care," I said again. Tears ran freely down my cheeks. I scraped the shaving cream off his back angrily, throwing handfuls of it onto the gray asphalt where it glowed in the gloom.

"Come on," he said when I had removed as much as I could. "Let's get some candy."

"I don't want to," I blubbered. "I'm going home."

"Don't be stupid." He was already heading toward Cascade Road, but I was rooted to the ground. I wiped the tears from my chin and clenched my jaw to soften the knot in my stomach. I watched him round the corner and disappear onto the larger street.

"Don't be boring," I muttered, running to catch up.

Now, watching a young family emerge from the jetway, I wonder about the appropriate number of anecdotes for a wedding toast. One? Two? More than that? Steven and I had been tight back then. We did almost everything together. He put up with me a lot more than *I* might have with a little brother. But I don't know what it means to be the big brother, only the little one. And when you're the little brother, it feels like you mess everything up.

"I said both record *and* play!" Steven snapped.

"It wouldn't go down."

"To save the computer program from the computer to the tape, you have to press both record and play. It didn't save so now we have to type the whole thing in again."

I looked down at the red button on the tape recorder as gray morning edged through the panes of the window beside us, glinting off the silver edges of the black plastic mesh protecting the tape recorder's speaker. I had read the program from the magazine while Steven typed it in. When we finished, it was supposed to be a race-car game. I didn't understand how it all worked, but he was 11 and I was barely 9.

"I thought you wanted to learn how to make a game," Steven said, exasperated.

I turned from the bare tree branches and patches of snow and brown grass in the front yard to the blank gray screen of the television. The tiny cursor blinked plaintively in the corner. My brother's new Commodore VIC-20 computer sat in front of it on a black and white folding TV table where it had been since he unwrapped it on Christmas Day.

"Keep it down." My dad appeared in the doorway to the den where he'd been sorting through bills. "You're going to wake up your mother," he barked louder than either my brother or me. He stood, glaring at us for a moment, and then turned back to the bills.

"It's too hard," I whispered. "Let's just play Omega Race."

"Everything's too hard for you," he said.

"Beating you at Omega Race isn't."

He flipped the magazine page back to the beginning of the program. "Let's type it again."

"It's boring," I said.

My mom appeared in the doorway from the stairs in a bathrobe, and shifted slowly toward the plaid yellow sofa behind us.

"Great job, guys," my dad yelled from the den before appearing in the doorway again. "Now turn that thing off."

"It's okay," my mom said. "My headache's gone."

"Go play with your Matchbox cars then," Steven said to me.

I turned and took a step toward the blue, green and red cars strewn across the throw rug between the sofa and Dad's scratchy brown chair.

"You're boring," I muttered under my breath.

"You're stupid," he muttered back.

"I don't want to hear another word from either of you," my dad snapped.

I settled in with the cars, and my brother turned back to the computer.

As I stood for boarding, I tried to remember when we stopped hanging out, playing Cities of Gold on his computer or going to church youth group together. There was a trip we made from Connecticut before moving back to Pennsylvania. We weren't sure yet if we were moving. I had told my folks I didn't care either way. They had put me in a private Christian school in Connecticut for seventh grade and I hated it, so I was ready to go. But a whole new state sounded a little scary. On the trip, we visited a charismatic church in Pennsylvania with a lot of dancing and speaking in tongues. We knew this was the type of thing that our parents really went in for and hadn't been able to find during our eight years in suburban Connecticut. Once the service started to get rowdy, we looked at each other and said, almost in unison, "It looks like we're moving." That was the last time I remember us being on the same page. Once we moved, I was quickly usurped by the pressures of middle school and at significant odds with my parents, who seemed to grow stricter with each passing day. By the next fall they'd found me a Christian school in Pennsylvania that I also hated, so the move hadn't really worked out the way I'd planned but, then again, not much does when you're thirteen.

One outing in particular sticks in my mind as a demonstration of how, even if you don't spend a lot of time together, you can still feel close. You can still learn something. It was the biathlon I'd entered with my brother in Dallas, Pennsylvania, our new home. He was doing the bicycling half of the event, and I was waiting for him to finish so that I could begin the footrace half.

As I lay back on the lawn beside the public library, a towering oak looming over me outlined against a white sky, the tension in my right hamstring made me wonder if it might have been a good idea to run a practice 5K before that day. Steven had been riding his bike several times a week, and although I was in decent shape for a fifteen-year-old and played sports regularly, I hadn't run much distance. A murmur ran across the small crowd watching the road in front of the bicycle finish line, and I sprang to my feet. I headed for the group of runners assembling at the start. My brother wasn't among the first group of riders to appear. *5K is nothing,* I told myself.

His yellow biking hat appeared at the top of the hill. He rushed toward me beside his best friend and cycling buddy, Jim. A hundred runners were already on the course, but with all the different age groups and categories, we still had a chance to place. The last thing I noticed was how tired he looked as he crossed the finish line, like he had given it his all. I felt elation as I burst onto the course. I set a brutal pace, thinking all the while about how the biathlon was the first thing we'd done together in a long time, maybe years. He'd been spending all his time with his band friends, and I was always cruising around in Mark's Vega or playing tennis. In a few months, he would graduate and head off to Wheaton College a thousand miles away. It felt good to do something with him again. I wondered if my parents pushed him to partner with me. It didn't make sense that he'd asked me and not one of his buddies. He must have had other options.

My legs started to ache as I hit the 2K mark, and I realized I'd been running too fast. I slowed a little, but my whole body was tightening up and I began feeling nauseous. At some point between the 3K and 4K markers, I got a cramp in my side. I never understood those guys who said to run through it. By the 4K mark,

I was walking. It felt good to catch my breath, a feeling that diminished as an old fat guy who I thought might teach English at the junior high passed me. When I came over the crest of the hill and saw the finish line ahead, I started jogging again. My brother stood with his friend Jim on the grass where I'd been stretching. I wished he'd gone home. I'd really let him down. I'd let everyone down. I was sure he was never going to do anything with me again.

I broke into a sprint and finished beside the old fat guy. Apparently he didn't pace himself, either. I fell onto the grass behind the finish line gulping air and trying not to hurl. My brother dropped to the grass beside me.

"I'm sorry," I said when I recovered enough to speak. "I started too fast."

"What are you talking about?" he said. "You finished."

I looked up at him and wondered how he could let me off the hook so easily. I would be punching him if he'd screwed up the race and I'd done well.

"I wanted to win," I said.

"Don't be stupid," he said. "It's just for fun. We were never going to win." It struck me that perhaps playing Dungeons & Dragons and working on the computer weren't the things that made him my big brother, and just because we had different friends and interests didn't mean I had to write him off.

"Don't be boring," I said, starting to think that I might avoid seeing my breakfast again.

The next fall, I was navigating a new high school alone, trying to fill the void he'd left inside of me with football buddies, girlfriends, house parties, whatever I could find. I often wondered if he felt the void, too. If he did, he appeared to fill it more with studying than anything else. He was one of the few pre-med students I knew who actually became a doctor. He always was smarter than me, even if I'm taller and better-looking. So that's a wash, right? I visited him at school once, then went to a different university, and the miles kept us apart. After graduation I ended up in Cleveland. He studied in Philly then interned in Harrisburg. Then he asked me to be his best man.

The rehearsal dinner and reception are at a private estate outside Harrisburg. Whitewashed fences surround a rustic farmhouse, natural wood with a dark gray finish and a matching barn that had been converted into an event hall. An occasional patch of shade moves across the green hills when a cottony cloud floats across the sapphire sky.

On this particular day, I watch my brother a lot. He seems happy, but with an air of anxiety that I'd never noticed before or at least given any thought to. But I'm anxious, too. The reception is pretty unstructured, and it's unclear when I'm going to give the toast. People are scattered about the estate, throughout the house and barn and on the sidewalks between, leaning on the white fences and chatting on the lawns. I wonder if my brother will be disappointed with the toast. Then I wonder if he'd ever been disappointed in me. If he had been, he'd never admitted it. But I don't want his wedding day to be the first time.

I spend the whole day looking for an opportunity to give the toast. I come close when a large group is gathered in the barn for the ceremonial first dance. I try to make my way to the emcee to ask for the mike, but I never quite get through the crowd, and they disperse or move onto some other activity, and I realize I've blown it again. My brother doesn't seem to care. Or I imagine it so.

As the sun slides closer to the green hill behind the farmhouse, the crowd thins and the shadows grow long. My brother's anxiety appears to wane with mine. I find a lonely spot with a blue wood-plank chair on the back porch facing that evening sun and loosen my bow tie. I pull out a sheet from the journal and read through the glowing accolades for my brother and his new bride I'd jotted down at the airport. As the sun touches the blades of grass on the top of the hill, my brother slips into the chair beside me.

"Whatcha doin'?" he asks.

"Just windin' down," I say.

He loosens his white bow tie and puts his feet up on the porch railing. I slip the sheet of paper into my pocket without reading through the second speech I'd written on the back. The one I would never give. Even if I had gotten my hands on that mike.

A big brother is always there

He defends you when the neighborhood bully chases you out of the bus and halfway down the street to beat the tar out of you because his sister doesn't like you

Even if the only thing he can do to defend you is scream at the bully that he's going to tell on him

He gives you countless rides to countless stupid events when your parents are too busy or just too annoying

He opens his bedroom door when you need to vent about your friends or lack thereof or girlfriends or any other stupid thing that little brothers vent about

If you're lucky, you get to share a room with him when you're younger

He listens

He talks

*He tells you the truth when you don't want to
hear it*

*He teaches you how to fight by kicking your
butt a couple times*

*And if you're really lucky you learn a thing or
two*

*When I think on it, being a big brother sounds
maybe a lot like being a husband*

So congratulations, Susan

*I hope he can be as good to you
as he's been to me*

Seth Roskos *lives with his wife and twin sons in Los Angeles, California. When he's not trekking through Joshua Tree National Park, a matrix of dingy Los Angeles alleyways or the Boulevard of Broken Dreams, he can typically be found belting out Katy Perry songs at the top of his lungs from the driver's seat of a red Prius, his vision blurred by tears of blissful grief.*

THE INTERRUPTION

Cindy McKay

THE DOORBELL STARTLED ME OUT OF A STUPOR. I'd been trying to figure out why the three trees in front of my house—each one filling a different pane of glass in the bay window—were all dressed for a different season: one green, one dead, one spitting its weary leaves at the other two.

I'd already decided that my favorite was the dead tree in the middle. Just roots and brown sticks. No soft green hope, no having to deal with loss. An existence without emotion, that's what I sought for myself. That's what comforted me, sitting in the middle of a wonderful life that kept coming at me. Happiness can be just as hard to live with as misery, maybe harder. With misery, you can spend your time searching for a cure. Happiness, on the other hand, doesn't require one. I was always looking for something to fix.

Whoever was at the door stuck his finger in the buzzer again, left it there for a few seconds longer than was necessary. He needn't have been so impatient, I was glad for the interruption. I hoped it would be the mailman, or the Schwan's man with his truck full of ice cream. I prayed it wouldn't be those black women who come around in pairs to hand out magazines about the end of the world. I always feel badly when they come, because I want to tell them that I don't really listen to a word they say. I want to tell them that they've been tricked into believing a lie, that I've had that glazed look in my eyes, too; that it's a lot easier to float downstream than it is to fight the current, but it sure makes for a dull ride. That they're only going to get angry at themselves for wasting so much precious time hiding from life when they should be enjoying every bit of it, even the filthy parts, *especially* the filthy parts. But I never say anything, I just nod and give them a quarter. I'm white and I'm guilty and I'm in the warm house drinking coffee while they're outside in their worn-out shoes, peddling doom. I hoped it wouldn't be them at the door.

It wasn't. It wasn't the mailman, either, or the ice cream man.

It was me.

It's funny how the sun disappeared the minute I opened the front door. The sun will do that, especially on windy days, when the light goes off and on as if someone is playing with the switch. I opened the door and the sun disappeared, and the wind stopped, too, or at least it stopped raining crisp maple leaves the color of toast.

I recognized myself right away, of course, even before I recognized the boy standing beside me. I was about eighteen, maybe already nineteen, but I looked like a girl of twelve. The swell of the belly was a dead giveaway, and so was the way I stood there, as if I thought I was invisible and no one would notice me at all. There was a terror in my eyes that I recognized, too. Not the kind of terror I feel now, when I know that life is good and that it could be taken away in the time it takes to miscalculate a yellow traffic light. This wasn't terror about understanding life, but just the opposite. This was a fear of not knowing what the hell life was, a very different kind of terror. The kind that enables you to grow up, or essentially go on, which is what growing up feels like when you look back at it. A blessing in disguise, until you see it again twenty years later and realize how cruel a joke eighteen, maybe already nineteen, can be.

"Can I help you?" I asked. Whatever could I be doing here on the front porch, especially with him, and after all this time?

He, of course, was the one to speak. At eighteen, I always let my husband do all the talking. After all, he was a big strong lug of almost twenty, too loud and too fearless, with muscles like inflated balloons captured beneath plaid flannel shirts. His hair was wild, the color of tarnished brass. His teeth were crammed in no particular order into his large mouth. His hands were greasy and oddly stubby, considering the rest of his overgrown anatomy. He smelled like the wind and spoke quickly, unaware of the way he abused the language.

"Me and her was asking all the neighbors around here if you want your leaves raked and bagged. No job's too big or too small."

His eyes were watery, wandered from place to place as if settling on one thing for too long was dangerous, or maybe just boring. Already he had looked past me into the house, back to the mailbox, the welcome mat, the street behind him, the porch floor where he impatiently tapped the flimsy prongs of his rusty blue rake. I remember ten years of trying to get his attention, and ten years of being ignored. It made sense, really. I didn't want to be seen, and he didn't look. We were perfect for each other, I could see that now.

There I was at his side, mute, obedient, thrusting my hips forward, not seductively, but to distribute the weight more evenly. I must have been about seven months pregnant. And I hadn't started biting my nails yet—they were still long and very clean. And my skin— God, it was so clear and smooth, there were no lines around the eyes, and that crease in my brow, the one my new husband is always trying to erase now with a gentle thumb and a reassuring kiss, well, it just wasn't there yet. Nothing was there but youth, awkward and unguarded.

"I don't imagine you've gotten much business around here."

The neighborhood was old but well-to-do. Most of the houses looked like ours, with its nine-foot windows and twenty-foot porch. Three stories of rooms we'd christened with pretentious names, a grand house as tall as it was wide, with pillars and stained-glass windows and ornate latticework that received a fresh coat of paint every other summer. It was awfully nice, I realized, *too* nice. I felt terrible, standing inside the doorway while they stood on the porch. How could they have known that I was in here, waiting? Somehow, I felt they had known.

"No, not much business," he said, studying the chipped paint on the handle of his rake, "I don't know why."

"It's Tuesday," I explained. Everyone was at work. Never mind that no one would hire them anyway, not when people had gardeners to rake their leaves.

While he moved his limbs restlessly, passing the rake from hand to hand, a mercenary in steel-toed boots anxious to be about the business of war, I noticed that I was standing perfectly still beside him, taking up as little space as possible to compensate. I was a mouse who'd been cornered, a fragile creature who believed that the only hope of survival lay not *within*, but in the merciful hands of *another*. That would change. Thank God, that was destined to change.

But for now, I, of course, would be responsible for raking the leaves—that I understood immediately. It would give him more power. He would stand there and say, "Christ, you rake like a moron," while he easily stuffed the bags with leaves, his giant arms working like bulldozers. I would have to pee and my back would ache from the pregnancy, but that wouldn't matter. I would want to tell him that he was stuffing the bags too full, that one of them was about to tear, but I would be afraid, and so I would remain silent. Also, we needed the money. He was apprenticed to a local plumber, barely making minimum wage. I would have recently quit my job as a receptionist, in preparation for giving birth. A receptionist, that's what I'd been for about eight months. A straight "A" student in high school, all that promise for the future, all those college applications I'd lost sleep over, those SATs I'd aced. And here I was, raking leaves to make up for the fact that my husband, a straight "D" student who had offered me a ride home after school one day, saying I wasn't just smart, I was pretty, too—well, he wasn't making enough money to pay the bills, and we didn't have any furniture in our apartment.

We had a window, though, I remembered that. It was a third-floor apartment, and at the front of the building was a bay window, not as tall or as beautiful as the bay window I'd been sitting at only moments ago, but still a great window. Rippled glass, white framework painted sixteen coats thick, and nothing behind me but an empty living room with a crib at the far end—but the rest of the world started with that window, and went on and on forever, right before my eyes.

I used to press my face up as tight as it would go against the glass, so close I could smell the Windex, warm and sharp inside my nose. It was the only window I ever washed. All the other ones looked out onto brick walls, but this one gave me a view of the entire hillside: tiny houses where people came and went, where people opened their mouths to speak to one another, but without sound. Even the cars made no sounds. It was like watching a silent movie. Little kids chased each other, and I imagined their screams. Rugs were shaken over porch railings and made *smack! smack!* noises inside my head. It was the backside of the neighborhood where everyone's gray underwear hung on wire laundry lines, where garbage cans overflowed and muddy shoes were abandoned by the kitchen door. It was colorless, soundless, and couldn't be touched, but it was wonderful to watch, the whole world to me.

I would sit for hours at that window, and stare, and wait. I don't know what I was waiting for, but I knew that whatever it was, it was out there. It surely wasn't in here, in this desolate apartment that smelled faintly of roach spray and the old people downstairs. Three tiny rooms were all we had, lined up right in a row so that you had to go through the bedroom to get to the living room. During those long days when he was at work, I would cradle my baby in my arms and wonder what it all meant, this desperate longing inside of me, the way I watched my life from somewhere else. I couldn't understand what I was doing here, in the middle of this terrible place, with my nineteen-year-old face pressed up against the window pane like a faded paper decoration taped to the glass when all along I had planned everything so differently.

And then his car would appear on that hillside—it was a Volkswagen Fastback, bright orange, the fenders spotted with brown primer like a rotting pumpkin—and I would watch that car wind its way down the hillside carrying my husband, my guide through this wilderness, home to me. My heart would soar at the idea of not having to be alone any longer. Even if he wasn't much company, he helped fill up some of the empty space that I always seemed to be drowning in. Until he took it up entirely, and I couldn't breathe at all.

If it was Friday, he would show up with a check for one hundred and forty-three dollars and some odd change. I would take it to the bank on Monday, but until then, it would be macaroni and cheese from a box and spaghetti with meatless sauce. Sometimes, I'd go see my mother and pretend it didn't hurt when she told me over and over again everything I was doing wrong, even the way I was holding my own baby. But at least I'd have a decent meal there, and a little security, while he was out partying with his friends. All the girls I'd known in high school were in college, wearing the latest fashions, experimenting with sex and drugs. I was a mother for the rest of my life. I never experimented. There were too many things to worry about.

"We could rake your leaves," he was saying now, "trim your hedges." He nodded towards the rhododendrons, which I had painstakingly and, to my great joy, successfully encouraged to grow from clay pots.

"I'm afraid I have someone who does that for me," I said, and instantly regretted it. He sucked on his cheek and looked away. But I'd always had a much harder time hiding my emotions. I watched the terror in my eighteen-year-old eyes turn into despair, could almost feel my insides start to quiver and my throat close up. *No, no, no,* I tried to stare into those eyes. *Anger is better, anger is like a thick, warm coat that insulates against whatever threatens, whatever it is, it doesn't matter. True, it can destroy you if you let it, but anger can also be very, very useful when you're eighteen and trying to make a living with a rake.*

I'd once used that anger to try punching him in the mouth. I'd been sitting up all night, waiting for him to return from another party. I'd just quieted the baby after she'd awakened from a bad dream, held her and told her it was alright, everything was fine, Mommy was here, not believing a word of it, but surprised at the calm in my own childish voice.

I'd returned to the kitchen, planted myself beside the refrigerator where I crouched in the darkness with both fists clenched. I didn't know which would have the better shot at his drunken face, but I knew that I would enjoy the sensation of crushing the cartilage in his nose with my knotted-up knuckles. Oh, I was going to let him have it, no chance of sweet-talking me under the sheets this time. I wasn't even going to give him a chance to open his mouth, just let loose with all my rage, right in his ugly, drug-swollen face, the minute he walked through the door.

But I'd fallen asleep back there, and when I woke up on the kitchen floor several hours later, he'd already come in and turned on the light. I heard the baby crying and the kink in my neck was unbearable, but it didn't hurt as much as knowing that I'd missed my chance. Delirious, I took a swing anyway, but he pushed me aside and my fist bounced harmlessly off his shoulder. I still remember the sound of him laughing, the sight of his wild face, hazy and blotchy-red against the stark, white walls of the kitchen. There was a pounding inside of me, like something was knocking, trying desperately to get out, and his laughs ripped into me like bullets until I was one giant, gaping hole.

I would hit my mark, finally, years later. One solid *whack!* to the jaw with the flat of my fist when he told me he was leaving me for another woman. It was a real letdown, after all that time. He just stood there and took it, and I knew then that punching him a thousand times wouldn't make me feel any better. I hated him for that, almost as much as I hated myself.

And yet there I stood now, on the front porch, full to bursting with the new, untarnished life that was growing inside me, still completely in awe of him, still willing to follow him to the ends of the earth and jump off if he asked me to. I could see that I hadn't learned yet, that I still believed everyone else's lies, hung on to everyone else's promises: his, God's, my mother's. *You would be smart to peel your face from that window pane now, stop waiting and get on with the anger, the sooner the better.* If only it had been those black women handing out magazines about the end of the world who had rung my doorbell.

"The thing is," I said, twisting my hands together, "it's just that…well, they came and raked the lawn yesterday." The yard was clearly green. Despite the leaves that had started to fall again, there weren't enough to fill even one bag, not even one of their generic brand plastic lawn bags.

Why didn't I just pay them twenty dollars, fifty dollars, a hundred dollars to rake my leaves? I had it, they needed it, life was so complicated. Why not say "okay" and soothe the ache in my heart?

I should have, I wanted to. But staring back in time, back into those eighteen-, maybe already nineteen-year-old eyes, I suddenly realized that there must have been some point in time when I stopped being her and started being me. Some line drawn down the middle of my life that separated us forever. The line that allowed me to stand here, looking out from inside the doorway of a safe place that I called home, from inside a loving marriage with a wonderful man. The line that allowed me to see that I had left my old self behind, that I had moved on, that I had survived, improved, no—excelled. Where was that line, I wondered? Just like the three panes of glass with three trees, each of which belonged in a different season: one green, one dead, one spitting its weary leaves at the other two. I was the spitting tree after all. Not green, not dead, but meant to shed my leaves and grow new ones, over and over again until I got it right. Over and over again. When would it stop?

"I'm sorry," was all I could think to say.

I watched the hope fall out of his broad shoulders, saw those eighteen-year-old eyes lose a little more life as I watched her lift a hand and absently caress her unborn baby. They stood there on the porch, and they didn't know what to do. They were trying as hard as they could, but it wasn't enough to make their lives better, it wasn't enough to keep her hand from shaking as she felt a tiny kick in her uterus and mouthed a silent prayer that love would be enough to raise her child. *It will,* I wanted to tell her, thinking of my own grown daughter. But she wouldn't understand that yet.

He lifted his rake then, and stuffed the lawn bags into her waiting arms. Without looking my way, he said that he saw, okay then, thanks anyway. He was always so proud, so determined. It made me feel a little better to see him square his shoulders again as he headed down the front steps. She trotted quietly behind. She didn't look back.

I went inside, closed two of the shutters, and watched the leaves fall silently, relentlessly, from the spitting tree to the green lawn below.

ॐ

Cindy McKay never set out to be a writer. She's a problem solver. To her, life is a series of knots that need to be untangled. There's nothing Cindy loves more than a big fat knot—the bigger the better. Fortunately, her life is full of them. Cindy's favorite way to untie knots is by writing stories and allowing her characters to work themselves free. They don't always succeed, but the joy for her is in the trying. She's never been content for longer than it has taken her to face the next glorious entanglement in her life, and discover the words that will unwind it. Cindy is a mother, a grandmother and a wife. If you wanted to, you could find her in a big old house in the East End of Pittsburgh, armed with a keyboard and a mouse, happily hacking away at the knots.

BECOMING MY MOTHER

John Highberger

WHILE I WAS ALWAYS AWARE THAT MY MOM had inspired me, it's only as I have crossed over the half-century mark that I realize how much she has done so, and how I am actually *becoming* her in so many ways. Whether I'm demanding my due or doing my duty, my mom has been an inspirational constant in my life. But the biggest impact, by far, was how she taught me to accept my own uniqueness in the face of daunting personal challenges.

One thing my mom always excelled at was getting what she had coming to her. I remember once when she was flying to visit my sister. My roommate and I had taken her to the airport and were waiting with her at the ticket counter at the gate (this was pre-9/11). When they announced that her flight had been canceled, I could see her blood start to boil. She approached the airline employee—my roommate and I slightly behind her, trying to keep up with her frantic pace—and demanded to know what was going on. "What do you mean the flight was canceled?" she said. "My daughter is waiting in Washington, D.C., to pick me up at the airport! They can't just *cancel* a flight!"

I tried to calm her down, saying, "Well, I guess there's nothing they can do."

"Well, they'll have to get me on another flight," she said. Which they promptly did. My roommate told me later that he thought my mom was going to jump over the ticket counter and attack the airline employee. He thought this was hysterical. I did, too, but only later. Much later.

I once had a similar issue with some work that I had done on my car. It took me *ten* trips to the auto repair shop, and after my dissatisfaction with their customer service, I wrote the national headquarters and received a *full* refund. My mom was flabbergasted that they reimbursed me, but since I was in the right, she was very proud that I stood up for myself and had my problem resolved.

Then there was another travel incident that needed to be taken care of. After my dad died, my mom and I began to take trips together. Our first two were to Canada and Mexico and went off without a hitch. We went to Bermuda for our third vacation and had another great experience—until we were checking out of our hotel. The clerk told us that we owed a few hundred dollars in "fees and taxes." We were never told of these charges by the airline we booked our trip through. Exasperated, my mom ended up writing a check for the amount, but when we returned, I told her that *I* would handle contacting the airline and, yes, you guessed it! I did receive a refund. Just like Mom taught me.

Now, my friends and I joke about me "pulling a Mrs. Highberger" from time to time when I go after a company like that.

While my mom always made sure to demand her due, she was also born in an era where people had a sense of duty toward how they lived their lives. There were things that folks were supposed to do and ways they were expected to act. My mom was no exception.

One day, an argument broke out between my dad and me. When I screamed at him, "I wish you were dead," my mom came racing towards me, telling me to "watch my mouth." To show you how fair she was, when my dad retorted with a comment, she went after him just as vehemently. I will *never* forget that moment, because it was one of the rare times that I feared my mom. Also, I felt badly. I had upset her, something I didn't like doing. She only wanted my dad and me to get along; she was playing the role of peacemaker—which she considered to be her duty.

Later that year, my dad passed away. He was 53 and died of a heart attack. I remember sitting in the hospital room, waiting for the doctor to come in. Once we learned of my dad's demise, my first thought, strangely enough, was, *Who will fix things around the house?* My older brother didn't live at home anymore, and I wondered to myself what would happen. My dad had taught me a lot about working on cars, but this seemed more daunting. At 18, I was now the man of the house.

Looking back, I realize that after my dad was gone, I never worried about the mortgage or having enough food to eat. With my mom now head of the household, all continued to be just fine. Eventually the mortgage got paid off, we remodeled some rooms in the house, and never once did it collapse on itself!

Years later, when she had an "empty nest," my mom mowed the lawn, kept small flower and vegetable gardens flourishing, trimmed hedges, washed and waxed her car, not to mention keeping the inside of her house spick-and-span. Guess who also likes a clean house? Yep, that would be me.

I'm always amazed at what anyone with a strong sense of duty does without thinking or hesitating. I'm speaking of things that just come naturally, things that you do because *instinct* tells you to do them. As everyone does, I've had my fair share of battles to wage. I dealt with asthma as a child and depression as an adult. I had a dream that I squelched for many years. My mom was there with me, each and every step of the way as I fumbled through life, searching for my own identity.

Many a night when I was growing up, wheezing and coughing from asthma, my mom and dad would sit in the living room with me. I was propped up with multiple pillows trying to breathe, and they would keep me calm, get me something to drink, and make a concoction of Vicks VapoRub and boiling water to ease my rasping. Whoever said being a parent would be easy?

When I was in my early twenties, I started feeling depressed. I didn't really understand what was going on, but I knew that something wasn't quite right. I hid it from most of the people in my life. A dear friend suggested I seek the help of a therapist. Not knowing what my mom would think, I finally told her what I was going through: the sadness, the crying late at night, the inability to sleep sometimes. She was one of the first people I told about my situation. When I told her that I was going to see a doctor about it, she didn't judge me. What I got instead was a loving mom's warm, sympathetic smile.

I started seeing a psychologist for weekly sessions. During the two years of therapy, I came out as a gay man—to myself, to my therapist and eventually to many of my friends. At first, I found it easier to tell people whom I wasn't close with. I guess I figured that if they abandoned me, it wouldn't matter as much. The first person I told was a guy I worked with, who then told me he was gay. Telling him was a *huge* weight off my shoulders. Nowadays, it's much more accepted in society. Back then, though, it wasn't as easy. I wasn't ashamed of who I was, but I was afraid of people turning their backs on me.

I remember a gay man visiting our family around that time, before I had come out to any of them. It was during the early days of AIDS, and there were many fears and unanswered questions. Someone said to my mom, "Oh, I'm so afraid we're going to get AIDS." My mom was livid. This comment just sent her over the edge. Without even knowing yet that I was gay, my mom retorted, speaking so quickly I could barely hear the words, "We don't even know if he has AIDS, and even if he did, there are only a couple of ways we could get it, and since we won't be engaging in those types of activities with him, there's no way we're going to get it!" That was the proudest I had ever been of my mom.

Gradually, the difficulty of coming out subsided, until the day arrived when I was doing some yard work at my mom's home and decided I wanted to tell her. At the end of the day, she was in the living room and I was in my bedroom. I wanted to tell her immediately, but I just couldn't find the right words, so I started crying. I don't know what possessed me to run into the living room, bawling like a child, but that's exactly what I did.

Upon seeing her adult son crying frantically, my mom practically jumped out of her skin and asked, "What's wrong?"

Stumbling and stuttering through many tears, I sobbed, "It's nothing really, and you probably already know, but I have something to tell you."

"Well, sit down and tell me what it is," she replied. When I told her I was gay, there was a pause for a few seconds (but in my mind, it felt like much longer) and she finally said, "Well, that's alright, but I had no idea."

I suddenly stopped sobbing and said, "You didn't? I just assumed you knew."

We then had one of the most heartfelt conversations we'd ever had. We talked about relationships, condoms (a first for us!) and the many other aspects of love. It was wonderful. I was accepted. Fully. Never judged.

It was also around this time that I realized my true passion in life: acting. I had always wanted to be an actor, but never did anything about it. I was 22 and saw an ad in the newspaper for adult acting classes at The Pittsburgh Playhouse. I'm a late bloomer with most things in my life, and this was no exception. I always felt that I wasn't good-looking enough to be an actor, and it took me a while to realize that not everyone in movies, TV and theater is magazine-cover material.

When my mom eventually came to see me in a show, she said, "You were really good!"

I was kind of surprised at her reaction since I'd been studying for three whole years. I responded, "Well, what did you expect? That I would suck?"

She said, "Well, I didn't know what to expect, but all I can say is that you were great!" She came to see that show and almost every one after that over the course of 11 years, before I moved away to Chicago.

One other area where I owe my mom gratitude is my spirituality. When I was a kid, we went to church every week (something I struggle with nowadays). I remember all the years I went to Sunday school and the day I finally was old enough to sit with her as a young adult during the service. I'd been taught by my Sunday school teachers to pray with my hands tightly clasped, but I can still see her praying as we sat in the pew, with just her arms crossed in front. I remember thinking, "How can she pray that way? That's not right." When I asked her about it, she told me that there is no correct or incorrect way to pray. What matters is what comes from your heart.

My mom and I were chatting once about religion, and I said to her, "I just don't believe that I'm going to hell because I'm gay."

She replied, "Well, of course not. I don't either."

Picture me. Beaming with pride. Again.

It may have taken me a while, but I realize that I wouldn't be who I am today without my mom. I found my love of a higher power, acting, travel—and acceptance of myself for who I am—largely through her. I also now have my own sense of duty. I try to be a good friend. I'm openly honest with people, no matter the relationship. I work hard at whatever I do and give it my all. I try to filter what I say rather than just blurt something out that I may regret later.

Oh, and in case you hadn't noticed, I don't take crap from anyone.

҂

John Highberger *was born and raised in Pittsburgh but moved to Chicago in 2000 to pursue his acting career in a larger market. At first intimidated by the sheer size of Chicago, he very quickly embraced his new home and is now thrilled to be living there. He recently completed a six-week course in stand-up comedy. He is looking forward to the coming year and what it has to offer in theatrical pursuits. He lives with his partner and their beautiful dog Lotus in an apartment with a view of Lake Michigan. Finally!*

THE GREATEST

Nicodemo Manfredo

IN THE AUTUMN OF 1989, I MET MUHAMMAD ALI. I'm sure he doesn't remember, and hasn't ever given the slightest thought to, that meeting. It was the first and only time I've seen him in person, but not the first time I learned something from him that changed the course of my life. We sat together on a stone bench in the woods in Farmington, Connecticut for three or four minutes, and in that time he only said five words. I think he said them to me. But he might have been talking to himself.

In 1964, 22-year-old Cassius Clay, later to be known as Muhammad Ali, beat the "Big Ugly Bear," Sonny Liston, for the heavyweight boxing title of the world. I was only ten, but I was aware of the fight because my family was into boxing. No one expected him to win. He was a 7-to-1 underdog, and everyone in my family and most people in my neighborhood, and most people in 1964 white America, didn't like him. He was "uppity." He was loud. He had an attitude of superiority and bluster that was unbecoming, and unacceptable, for a black man. We didn't refer to them as black at the time. Or colored either. We expected "our" Negroes to be quiet and dignified and suitably polite. Like Joe Louis. Or Floyd Patterson. Or, ironically, like Sonny Liston, who was sullen, scary and connected to organized crime. But quiet was important. Liston wasn't uppity. Or flashy. Or loud. We were okay with the other stuff because it wasn't aimed at us and because we didn't feel disrespected and threatened.

Clay, on the other hand, threatened us right through our TVs. He didn't conform to what we expected of him. My father, Pap—a brutal, violent and racist man, who was very knowledgeable about boxing and had never lost a bet on a fight—claims now that he always loved Clay (although he refused to refer to him as Ali until most of the world didn't even remember his "slave name" anymore). But I remember it differently. Before Liston, in fact since he came to national attention by winning the gold medal as a light-heavyweight in the 1960 Summer Olympics, Dad and his boys would discuss at length how this guy (Clay) was pretty good, but whoever the next fight happened to be against was gonna shut the uppity bastard's mouth for good.

"Uppity" was used a lot, but never to describe white people.

Clay's first fight with Liston ended with a technical knockout when Liston couldn't answer the bell for the seventh round. It was a shock. Clay jumped up on the ropes yelling, "Eat your words! Almighty God was with me. I want everyone to bear witness, I am the greatest! I'm the greatest thing that ever lived. I don't have a mark on my face, and I upset Sonny Liston, and I just turned twenty-two years old. I must be the greatest. I showed the world. I talk to God every day. I know the real God. I shook up the world, I'm the king of the world. You must listen to me. I am the greatest! I can't be beat!"

That was the first time I remember realizing that Pap— who would never have been mistaken for a "good man" and who didn't allow any argument, discussion or contradiction by *anyone*—was wrong. And it was a black man who had proved him wrong. I didn't care all that much about Clay beating Liston, but he got away with making Pap wrong. *That* was a victory. To me, *that* was greatness.

Clay joined the Nation of Islam, which we called "The Black Muslims," changed his name and, as Muhammad Ali, defended his title in a rematch against Liston. Pap and the boys knew The Bear was gonna eat him up in this one. But before the people in the most expensive ringside seats had even made their dramatic hierarchy of entrances, the fight was over. The "phantom punch" had knocked Liston out in two minutes of the first round. Of course there was controversy. It must have been a fix. The knockout punch was almost invisible. Ali had knocked Liston out while backing away. Nearly impossible. The rumors of Liston "going in the tank" (deliberately losing the fight) started immediately. People said: "The Black Muslims, The Nation of Islam, threatened him." "He took a dive to pay off gambling debts." Modern technology shows the truth: a chopping right hand from Ali, so fast that the frame speeds on the cameras of the day were barely able to catch it clearly. He had beat both Liston and Pap twice.

With every fight, he became more of an irritation to most whites. Because he got louder and smugger and more blustery and more vain and more threatening and more *uppity.*

His second title defense was against former heavyweight champion Floyd Patterson. Ali didn't have anything personally against Patterson until Patterson made a disparaging remark about Islam. Patterson was well-liked, good-looking, polite, nice (and not at all uppity). Ali made fun of him. He called him a white man's champion. During the fight, Ali taunted Patterson, embarrassed him. He refused to even throw a punch in the first round, instead just dancing around and making Patterson look bad. Ali deliberately dragged the fight out for 12 rounds and TKO'd Patterson in the 12th. The sportswriters and reporters criticized him for it. Said he was "unsportsmanlike." Ali said, "I ain't gonna be the champ the way you want me to be the champ. I'm gonna be the champ the way I wanna be. I know where I'm going and I know the truth, and I don't have to be what you want me to be. I'm free to be what I want."

It was 1965. I was 11 years old. I lived in an all white, blue-collar, run-down area of Pittsburgh called Greenfield. I was in 6th grade in an all-white Catholic school. I had never met a black person. Had never seen a black person close up except for the "garbage men" who picked up the trash every week.

Growing up, I was taught every negative stereotype about black people, and I believed them all. I was told that black people were dirty and lazy. That they didn't work. That they lived in the projects on welfare and didn't believe in family life like we did. Meanwhile, I lived in an abusive home, in subsidized housing, on welfare. My father lived with us only sporadically. Our house was so dirty and roach-infested that, today, I'd hesitate to walk into it. I was told that black people were stupid and uneducated. The only reading material in our house was porn and white supremacist magazines and newsletters. Very few people in my family completed high school.

Ali's next fight was supposed to be against Ernie Terrell. Terrell was the WBA (World Boxing Association) heavyweight champion because that organization had stripped Ali of his title after he joined the Nation of Islam and refused to register for the draft. In 1964, as Clay, he was classified as 1-Y (available only during national emergency or declared war) because of his poor reading and spelling skills. In February of 1966, he was reclassified to 1-A (available for service). He refused: "I ain't got nothing against no Viet Cong. No Viet Cong ever called me nigger. Why should they ask me to put on a uniform and go ten thousand miles from home and drop bombs and bullets on brown people in Vietnam while so-called Negro people in Louisville are treated like dogs and denied simple human rights?"

I was 12 now. Until that moment, the words—the actual words—"civil rights" had always meant, in my neighborhood at least, "black people rioting to take stuff away from white people who had worked hard for it." Vietnam had been in the news for as long as I could remember, and I wasn't clear on what it was. My perception was that the Vietnamese weren't Americans and they weren't white and they must have done something to us or we wouldn't be over there. I had cousins and people I knew from the neighborhood over there, but I didn't really get why. Until I heard Muhammad Ali say those words, it had never clicked with me that the words meant something real. He had already "whupped" my father enough times that I really believed he was something out of the ordinary. He said he was the greatest and no one believed him, but he proved it every time he said it. He was the highest-paid athlete in the world.

He was the best at what he did. He lived by rules that *he* made for himself.

Ali had everything. His words affected me because he—the greatest—was openly, clearly and unapologetically willing to give up everything because he believed in *something*. Ali's attitude made me realize that I wasn't supposed to simply accept that what the people I was afraid of said was true. It made me realize that it was *my* responsibility to find the truth, the validity, before I committed myself to something. It made me want to be sure of what was right and what was wrong and what I condoned and condemned. It made me want to be brave and moral and strong enough to do what I believed was right. It made me a different person.

After his refusal to go to Vietnam, Ali's license to fight was systematically revoked in state after state. It was a struggle to find a place that would sanction an Ali fight. The fight with Terrell didn't happen until 1967 in Houston. The fight was famous for its brutality and for Ali's technical brilliance. Ali won a 15-round decision.

Shortly after the Terrell fight, Ali was stripped of his titles, convicted of refusing to register for selective service, sentenced to five years in federal prison and fined $10,000. His legal and financial battles were just beginning. He didn't fight again until the late 1970s. He was sidelined from the time he was 25 until he was 29 years old. In boxing, these ages are a fighter's prime. But even though he was financially ruined, he never slacked in his convictions. And he never shut up. He never got quiet. He said, "Only a man who knows what it is like to be defeated can reach down to the bottom of his soul and come up with the extra ounce of power it takes to win."

In 1971, the U.S. Supreme Court overturned his conviction. During his suspension from boxing and the appeal process, opposition to the Vietnam War began to grow and his position on it gained public sympathy. He spoke at colleges and universities against the war and in promotion of civil rights, African-American pride, and racial and social justice.

Ali went on to be the first person to win the heavyweight championship twice. Then later, a third time. He was in his thirties, geriatric for a boxer. His mantra had always been "float like a butterfly, sting like a bee." He was famous for damaging flurries of punches that could barely be seen. He was just as famous for the "Ali shuffle," where he'd dance a kind of a fast jig in the middle of the ring, shuffling his feet in place in rapid succession like a dancer.

By 1974, much of his former speed and flash, the things that boxing fans contended won his fights, were largely gone. He was never known for being able to *take* big punches. He was known for being able to avoid being hit. He developed a new strategy, as usual controversial, even among his own trainers. It was called "rope-a-dope." He'd allow the hardest punchers in the heavyweight division to get him into a corner against the ropes—a suicidal strategy—and throw their hardest punches at him while he feigned fatigue and helplessness. He'd take the dangerous punches on his elbows and shoulders until his opponents ran out of energy, then he'd slip off the ropes and win the fight.

The point, what *I* saw, was not that he was great at boxing (which, of course, he was). It was that he was great at taking whatever strengths he had at the time to reframe the moment. To turn it into what *he* decided it would be. It was the way he had taken the hated "uppity black man" and turned it into a dignified, powerful human being who wouldn't be enslaved. When he was fast, mentally or physically, he used the speed against the slow hands, feet and wits of his opponents and detractors. When he was slow, he turned *that* into a power that stymied the younger and stronger. He said, "Champions aren't made in the gyms. Champions are made from something they have deep inside them—a desire, a dream, a vision."

In October of 1980, Ali was 38 years old and came back from a short retirement—largely for financial reasons—to fight Larry Holmes, a former sparring partner. Ali lost in the 10th round when his manager "threw in the towel." It was his last time in the ring. I was in my twenties. We watched on closed-circuit TV. Even the people who would have lost money on their bets wished he had won, or at least that he had lost in a better way. He looked old and tired and beaten and embarrassed. Holmes, his opponent, kept asking the ref to stop the fight. Ali had been *his* hero, too.

Shortly after the Holmes fight, there were rumors that Ali was sick. Some said the last fight against Holmes had done serious damage to him. People who knew better, knew better. He hadn't taken a brutal beating in the ring that night. We all realized that 20+ years in the boxing ring against some of the toughest men in the world eventually took their toll on even the most resilient bodies and brains. In 1984, it was made public that Ali was suffering from Parkinson's syndrome, an incurable disease most likely caused by the years of head trauma. His head and hands shook. His speech was stuttery and slurred.

Still, he remained outspoken and cheerful and stayed in the public eye in various capacities. Doing charity work, promoting the causes he had always promoted. I avoided seeing him on TV. It was too hard for me to see someone who had been the embodiment of victory over impossibility. I wanted to remember him as who he was then, not who he is now. I didn't want to see proof that, even if we approached trials with perfect courage and confidence and strength and purity of spirit, we could still get defeated.

I am a musician. It's what I do for a living. With few exceptions, it's what I've always done for a living. I never made the decision that this was what I was going to do. I've just always known that it's the only thing that I identified with. That it's me. I've never "made it big." It's never been an easy way to make a living. But it's me. I have a friend who wrote a song called "Life in a Cup." The first line is: *Some people say I ain't never gonna make it. Well I don't know. I think I make it every day.* That sums it up for me.

The success isn't the money or the recognition. The success is knowing what's right for you (a hard thing in itself) and doing it. Like Ali. This is who I am. This is what I do. I do it because in *my life,* not only do I *get* to make the decision, but it's my responsibility. Not to be selfish or to not care about others, but to give my friends and my family and myself the real person who lives in here.

In 1989, my life was a wreck. I was 35 years old. I had been married for 11 years. I had bought a small house and a new car. I had tried for so long and with so much effort to keep doing music for a living, but it was a struggle to keep up with the mortgage and household bills and find steady work as a musician during economic upturns and downturns. It was also difficult to keep a marriage working while spending long weeks on the road. Spending nights working in bars didn't help, either.

I've always been good at technological things, an ability that came from the necessity of working on amplifiers and mixing boards during performances and working on junk cars in the middle of the night in the middle of someplace on the way to someplace else. So five years before, in 1984, I had taken a job using some of those skills. It was steady work. Doing computer tech stuff in the days when computers were just becoming a necessity to business was a good way to make money. It took a lot of pressure off the financial part of life. But I was profoundly unhappy with who I had become. I didn't identify with the life I was living. I felt like I was cheating on myself. It's not an exaggeration to say that, when I was the most secure financially and making the most money I had ever made in my life, I *hated* who I had become. And now I was trapped in the financial responsibility of security and keeping the money flowing. I was hanging on to the parts of being an artist that I had time for: drinking, drugs and cheating on my wife. I felt dirty and dishonest and trapped and weak and defeated and out of ideas.

I had been working on a technology project outside Hartford, Connecticut. I'd been staying at the Marriott for about a week. The hotel was in a business park surrounded by woods crisscrossed with walking trails. I'm a big "woods" guy. On my second day there, Muhammad Ali arrived at the hotel on a tour to promote a new cologne. It was called "Ali." For the rest of the week, I saw him several times a day from a distance. I never approached him because I was feeling depressed and hopeless, and I didn't want to risk seeing him in the same condition. He carried a packet of pamphlets from the Nation of Islam. They were pre-signed:

"To _____ from Muhammad Ali."

On my last night of the project, I packed the car, had dinner at the hotel, went out with some colleagues. At about 2 a.m., I was getting ready for the drive back home, a few hours away. Before leaving, I decided to take a walk through the woods to clear my head. While I walked and thought, my eyes filled and I started to cry. And then there he was. He was leaning on a stone bench on the path. He was big, 6'3", maybe 250 pounds. Gray-haired. He didn't say anything, but he reached into his pocket and pulled out the packet of pamphlets. His hands seemed slow but not very shaky.

I wiped my eyes and said, "Sorry." Then I turned to walk away. But I turned back and said, "I don't want to interrupt or intrude, and I don't need an autograph. I just wanted to say there's only ever been one greatest. And that's you." And I got all choked up and started to cry again. He sat on the stone bench and patted the seat next to him. I sat. Embarrassed. We sat there for three or four minutes. Neither of us said anything. Then he stood up, didn't look at me, just at the ground, and did a slow and clumsy "Ali shuffle," threw an equally slow and clumsy left jab/left hook/right uppercut and said:

"How 'bout one more comeback."

Nick Manfredo *was born in 1954 in Pittsburgh, Pennsylvania, into a family of questionable character, and lived there until he graduated high school in 1972. A lifelong professional musician, Nick's first instrument, a guitar, was provided by his uncle Billy. Billy, a member of the family business—larceny—had asked Nick what he wanted for Christmas. Nick replied, "A chemistry set." Billy's answer was, "Where in the hell am I gonna steal a chemistry set? You're getting a guitar." Nick left Pittsburgh after graduating high school, living and traveling extensively in the U.S., Ireland and Canada. He began to keep journals and write stories while playing in a bar band in Belfast, Northern Ireland, during the height of the "Troubles" in 1974. He now lives in Boston.*

Would you like to learn
more about our authors?

Do you want to buy
a book for a friend?

Are you just plain nosy?

Visit us at

WWW.DAMMITBOOK.COM